The World Is Listening to Steve Santagati . . . Are You?

"I wish this book had been written fifteen years ago. It would have helped me so much through my high school and college years. Thank you for allowing us a peek into a guy's mind. Your book is not only educational but very entertaining to read. It definitely left me wanting more!"
—*Jeena, USA*

"I read your book, *The Manual*. It was informative and gut-wrenchingly funny; I laughed so much I cried. It is rare to see someone who is not afraid to go against the grain, think outside the box, be their true authentic self. . . . It is refreshingly appealing."
—*Renu, USA*

"I just finished reading your book, which I really enjoyed. I even admit to not wanting to put it down. Thanks for sharing your words of wisdom. A lot makes sense to me now—I wish I had this book about ten years ago!"
—*Paula, Canada*

"Your book is great! You are heaven-sent for us women who cannot decipher the codes that men always send."
—*Alma, Ireland*

"I have read your book and I loved it. The messages are presented in a funny way that's never boring. It's fun reading it even when you don't need any relationship advice."
—*Asmara, Indonesia*

"I must say I laughed my ass off about a lot of it because it covers just about every guy I have ever dated . . . and now I feel like I am a little of the bad girl, which is kind of exhilarating. I have thoroughly enjoyed the book; it will now become my point of reference."

 — *Tracey, Australia*

"You won me immediately with your honest, light-spirited approach, wit, and irresistible charm and charisma. I ordered your book from Amazon and it is my bedtime reading."

 — *Dafne, Croatia*

"Your book will be the bible that I will read over and over and refer on to my single friends! Keep up the great work . . . we women want to know everything."

 —*Kym, Australia*

The Manual

A True Bad Boy Explains How Men
Think, Date, and Mate—and What
Women Can Do to Come Out on Top

STEVE SANTAGATI

with Arianne Cohen

 Three Rivers Press
New York

Published in the United States by Three Rivers Press, an imprint of the Crown
Publishing Group, a division of Random House, Inc., New York.

www.crownpublishing.com

Three Rivers Press and the Tugboat design are registered trademarks of Random
House, Inc.

Originally published in hardcover in the United States by Crown Publishers,
an imprint of the Crown Publishing Group, a division of Random House, Inc.,
New York, in 2007.

Library of Congress Cataloging-in-Publication Data
Santagati, Steve.
  The manual : a true bad boy explains how men think, date, and mate—and what
women can do to come out on top / Steve Santagati.
      p. cm.
  1. Men—Psychology.   2. Dating (Social customs).   3. Man-woman relationships. I. Title.

HQ1090.S326 2007
646.7'7082—dc22   2006034128

ISBN 978-0-307-34570-7

Design by Lauren Dong

First Paperback Edition

146122990

This book is dedicated to every woman who flirted with me, slept with me, slapped me, beat me at my own game, broke my heart or my ego, taught me "how to" and "how not to." To every woman who understood me—who, in spite of myself, forgave me, dumped me, loved me, took care of me, befriended me, or tortured me. This book is dedicated to every curve of a woman's body, every lock of hair, every mischievous smirk, soft hands, lingerie, foreign accent, scream of outrage, sensitive vulnerability, beautiful kiss, warm hug, every body type out there, and everything that makes women the most beautiful creatures to look at and be around on the planet.

Contents

Part V   **MATING**

Early in the Game

End Game

Game On!

Part VI   **Q&A**   **281**

Introduction

The pages you're about to read reveal everything that you need to know to successfully date and have relationships with men. I'm going to tell you how men think, date, and mate, so that navigating the dating world will become as easy as changing a lightbulb: just toss out the old one, grab a new one, and screw him . . . in.

I am a Bad Boy coming clean: I'll explain everything that Bad Boys have been hiding for a very long time—our private secrets of dating. Ten years ago, you never could have gotten it out of me, because the first rule of being a Bad Boy is: never talk about being a Bad Boy. We hide behind our charm and charisma, all while exercising our cunning understanding of the female mind. But after almost three decades of experience, I am ready to share the secrets of our trade.

I'm confessing in order to teach you everything you need to know to break the male code in relationships. In mere hours, you will no longer be wondering what he's thinking, and you'll have the upper hand in the dating game once and for all. Turns out you *can* change your man into a committed and loving boyfriend—or husband—but first you have to change the way *you* think about the male-female dynamic.

So, why me? Why am I the authority? Well, what distinguishes me from everyone else is my ability to put this information into language that makes sense and, therefore, allows you to actually use it! Sounds simple, but it's not. Next time you're watching a relationship segment on television or reading a self-help book, ask yourself if you can really take what the "expert" is telling you and use it that night in your own life. Probably not. But this isn't just another relationship advice book; it's *The Manual*! Your DVD player came with instructions; don't you think it's worth reading the instruction Manual on men?

You may be wondering how I am able to put such useful information in your hands. Well, my life has been full of female influence, beginning with my growing up in a houseful of girls, having loads of female roommates, and then, of course, juggling a girlfriend or two (or two hundred). I've always told my female friends what guys were up to, straight from the hip. Sometimes they looked at me like dogs hearing a funny noise; they didn't fully grasp what I was trying to say. I realized that no one had ever told them the straight-up truth before in a way they could comprehend. Men and women speak a different language. Think of me as not only your advisor, but also your translator.

Now, if you prefer reading relationship books written by psychologists, fear not: A Ph.D. candidate studies for between four to six years. I've been "studying" the seduction of women for more than twenty-five years. I have the equivalent of four doctorates in this field. And let's face it, there is no substitute for real-life experience and street smarts. None!

You don't even need to love Bad Boys to learn from this book. You just need to love men. Understanding a Bad Boy—the best of the worst—is a great way to understand all us guys. All guys have similarities; chances are, any man you desire, whether he's a banker or a baker, will have some degree of bad surging through his veins. Besides, that nice guy you're after might not be so nice after all. Also, the badder we are, the less you realize it. When I started working on this book, I ran into ex-girlfriends who laughingly blurted out, "You're not a Bad Boy." Success! True Bad Boys are wolves in sheep's clothing. You need to be alert, ladies: just because he's not covered in tattoos doesn't mean he's not bad.

All of this begs the question "How can this book change my life?" Two ways:

1. Ninety percent of the so-called relationship experts on TV or in the glossies are only putting Band-Aids on relationship wounds. They're not teaching women how to read men well enough to enter hot, healthy relationships. If you listen, a man will tell you everything you need to know about how he feels about you, what he's doing, what he's planning next. I will teach you how to read these signs.

2. Women who truly understand men can beat them at their own game, and take the shortcut to finding happy relationships. It is possible for *all women* to wrap their minds around Bad Boy behavior, and use it to their advantage in any relationship. I will teach you how to do this. It's a question of mental empowerment, allowing *you* to call the shots, which will change the way you live and love.

Courting is like a dance: men lead and women follow. But wait—that kinda sucks, because most men just "lead" you into bed and stop dancing before the song is over, in more ways than one. Proactive women, on the other hand, step on some toes when necessary and make that dance last for years. This book will help women be proactive by providing them with the truth and the knowledge—the *power*—to lead a relationship in whatever direction suits them.

My aim in this book is unlike that of any relationship advice book out there: To get you to understand that dating is about carrying yourself with a new, confident understanding of the way mating works. To get you to understand that dating is not about picking someone up or manipulating him. It's something to study, soak in, and store in the back of your mind. It's something that should become a part of you, something you'll draw on later when you seize every opportunity, take charge, and meet men face to face as often as possible.

There are going to be some chapters in here that will be tough to swallow. But rest assured that, in those chapters, I am telling you the truth about men and relationships and giving you information that can only help you. I guarantee you'll be in awe of the changes you see in your dating life if you take the time to read this book and apply it to every Mr. Right who comes along.

Part I

The Heart of the Bad Boy

The first step toward enjoying your man is understanding exactly who you're dealing with. In this first part, we'll go over the ins and outs of who a Bad Boy is, why he's the way he is, and how to spot him before he spots you. I'll also show you that bad is the new good, reveal how not to be fooled by imitation Bad Boys, and teach you to figure out which of the many men from the playing field you're dealing with.

Chapter 1

Who Is a Bad Boy?

Admit it, you want to date Bad Boys. Despite what your mother may have told you, we make the best boyfriends. We're fun, we love women, and we know how to turn you on. Let me explain.

Bad • Boy (n.) A charming, funny, overtly confident guy who is sexy, in good shape, and great in bed (like I said, overtly confident). He is unapologetically "male," loves women, maintains many female friends, and *does not kiss and tell*. Romantically, he gets away with murder, with an alibi of a wink and a smirk. He's noncommittal by choice, not by fear. Most important, he thrives on being naughty.

I'd be sugarcoating the definition, however, if I didn't explain the "bad" part. He's bad because he's "got your number," knows how to manipulate you, and might not view female casualties as a problem. He doesn't always see you as a person, but instead as a challenge or a case study. For many Bad Boys, the chase is more important than the catch. The outcome? Hearts are broken, your need for closure is ignored, and he's off to his next "mark," remembering you only as an experience. If that's not bad, what is?

Examples: Great Hollywood Bad Boys have included Colin Farrell, George Clooney, Jack Nicholson, Johnny Knoxville, Jude Law, Snoop Dogg, Warren Beatty, Vince Vaughn, and (yes, really) John Mayer. (The sensitive guitar players are brilliant; you'll never see them coming.)

My point is that Bad Boys come in all shapes and sizes. I used to think that only tough guys were Bad Boys, but I was wrong; they're often the earthy types, the businessmen, and the boys next door.

You know when a Bad Boy enters a room: His confidence and past success with women are revealed in his unflinching eye contact, his slow, definite pace, and the glaring looks he receives from other men. Meanwhile, the women in the room perk up like deer at a water hole. He is automatically king of whatever domain he enters, and he doesn't feel the need to prove himself. He just *is*.

Dedication to the Cause

A Bad Boy studies women with the same passion and dedication that Nobel laureates pursue academia. A Bad Boy receives equally impressive rewards . . . albeit not in the form of medals and plaques. Instead, he gets something better, something every man on the planet desires: an undeniable ability to seduce women based solely on *who he is*. Women are attracted not to his status, bank account, or intellect; instead, he can woo women strictly based on *himself*. (Why? We'll get to that in the next section, "Why You Have No Choice but to Like Us.") For a man, there is no bigger ego boost than having a woman fall weak in the knees because of his effect on her. It's our most primitive quest.

Most true Bad Boys are born or reared as such. On occasion, a lucky few stumble and accidentally fall into behaving badly as a route to success with the opposite sex, summoned to a life spent pursuing the understanding of women. Either way, we leave no stone unturned when it comes to girls. We want to know everything, from why you get edgy during PMS to why you enjoy sex, as well as what makes you laugh, what your weaknesses are, how to build you up and how to knock you down a few pegs, and what makes you happy.

Why You Have No Choice but to Like Us

There have been all sorts of studies done on why women are attracted to this "naughty" element in men. To us Bad Boys, this is all just scientific chatter. However, I have taken the time to examine sociological and anthropological research on the topic, and it comes down to this: A desire to propagate is rooted deep within our species. Along with that desire, we have biological traits that guide us in choosing the right mate. Women have the best chance at propagating if they choose only the strongest alpha males, and men have the best chance of propagating if they can attract many females. You see this in nature all the time.

But humans have reached a level of civilization that doesn't admire the male side of that equation. Polygamy went out with the corset, hence the conundrum in dating. Bottom line? You like me, want my romantic attentions, and want me to date you monogamously. And there's nothing you can do to keep me from playing the field. Or is there?

Keep reading, because even if you think you don't like full-blown Bad Boys, every woman needs a guy with an edge to keep her heated up. The following pages will help you keep that fire burning—and under control.

Chapter 2

Who He's Not

I hear the word *player* tossed around a lot to describe men who seek out hordes of women. This is accurate. But I'm here to break it down for you, and tell you that Bad Boys and players are *not* the same thing. Let me explain:

Player	Bad Boy
Brags about his conquests	Is very secretive, and will rarely talk about his private life
Cares deeply about his "numbers"	Enjoys exploring many "types" of women
Has a sleazy air	Is confident
Makes a sport out of getting women's phone numbers	Absolutely loves women
Has a shallow understanding of women, and cares to know only enough to get them into bed	Most of his ex-girlfriends are still his friends and not wishing for his untimely death

In a nutshell, a player sees women as notches on his bedpost. He doesn't really like them, or care to understand them. A player prefers to get women drunk and take advantage of them. He doesn't care *how* a woman is seduced, as long as she goes to bed with him. He sees women as something of a sport. Most players are wealthier men who prey on gold diggers, drunk girls, or unsuspecting women. But a player can easily be the unemployed loser down the block—Lord knows he has the time. If you want to know what to look for in order to avoid this guy, pay attention here.

How to Spot a Player

- He has more male than female friends.
- He may have cash and fancy "props": watches, cars, and clothes.
- He's a name-dropper.
- He makes promises he never keeps.
- He begins touching you—your back, your arm, anywhere—from the moment you meet, in ways that might strike you as far more intimate than your relationship warrants.
- You'll think something about him is sleazy, even if you can't put your finger on it. Should you put your finger on it, please wash with hot, soapy water.

Players can eventually be turned into good guys, but it's better to know what you're dealing with from the get-go. Chances are, though, you aren't going to be the one to change him, so move on quickly if you want to avoid the heartache.

A Word on Misogynists

A *misogynist* is a man who dislikes women. I'm not a psychologist, so I can't give you a clinical character description, but suffice it to say, this is a man who fundamentally doesn't respect the opposite sex. These losers often have disturbing pasts, for one reason or another, whether it was a childhood trauma or merely how they were raised.

Misogynists work many of the same moves as players. But the line between a player and a misogynist is a thick one. When meeting a man, look for the distinct sense that he doesn't like you even though he's attracted to you; he may also make negative comments about female family members. You'll know it when you sense it. Some misogynists can also be abusive—any man who is verbally or physically abusive, whether he harms you or threatens to do so, is to be avoided. Players may be derogatory at times, but your feminine instincts won't tip you off to danger the way they will if you're with a woman hater. These idiots do not deserve your pity and should be avoided at all costs. It is these violent, derogatory, sexist pigs who are a disgrace to our species. As much as I don't think players are cool, even they don't sink to a misogynist's level.

Be careful out there, and trust your instincts! If you're out on the town and meet a man, take a ladies'-room break and review the situation. Be honest with yourself, and you'll know exactly what kind of guy you're dealing with. The player will check out your girlfriend, and the girl behind her, when he introduces himself. The misogynist will come on way too nice, and you'll get a creepy feeling. He will most likely offer to buy you a drink (something he can drug). The Bad Boy, however, will start talking to you as if he knows you—with a calm self-assuredness—and you won't even know he's trying to pick you up until you're leaving his apartment the next morning with your panties in your purse.

Chapter 3

The Myth of the Nice Guy

I can hear you disagreeing with me. "But, Steve," you say, "I don't like Bad Boys. I really don't."

Bull.

If only the world were perfect. Nice girls would fall in love with nice boys, and everyone would live happily ever after. (Insert record scratch here.) Nothing could be further from the truth. Odds are you'll never fall for a plain old nice guy.

That's not to say that you won't meet an edgy guy who is nice to you. Or that you won't become attracted to an extremely courteous guy. But, inevitably, the *je ne sais quoi* about him that makes you want to jump his bones is not his habit of helping you on with your coat. You prefer his overt confidence when he's helping you off with your skirt.

In that world called reality, every guy has a little Bad Boy in him, and women wouldn't have it any other way.

There's Nothing Nice About Nice

A nice guy is the boy you want to pat on the head like a puppy, saying, "Aww, aren't you sweet." He's probably the friend whom you adore but would never date. Nice guys can't get you hot. Nice guys can't even "get" you. Nice guys, as far as women are concerned, may as well have WELCOME stamped across their foreheads, because you use them as doormats. Which is sad, because a lot of nice guys would make great boyfriends, except for one thing: They don't make you feel safe. Or excited.

The same reason nature instructs you to go for an alpha male is why you can't be attracted to "nice." In nature, nice equals weak, and weak equals danger. Women want to feel that they're protected and safe. Even if you're a powerful woman, you still want to be with someone who's got some balls. No?

But I'm Over Bad Boys

Maybe you say you're over Bad Boys. You say that you want to settle down and meet someone nice. What, you can't sleep? You need someone around to bore you into a deep slumber? Predictable nice guys can have that NyQuil effect.

Come on, sweet cheeks, you don't want that. Wanting a nice guy is the number one sign that you're *settling*, and not looking for the best you can get! But if you agree with me on that, now you're really stuck. You don't want nice and you don't want bad. What to do?

Here's how to zero in on a guy with just the right amount of Bad Boy–ishness.

1. Date different types of guys from various walks of life: business types, creative, athletic, outdoorsy, etc. (but don't sleep with any of them . . . unless one of them is me. . . . Joking, sort of.)

2. Especially date outside of what you would consider your normal "type," and start to form an idea of what you like and don't like; keep a chart, if it helps. Ask yourself what qualities are most important to you. Is he polite? Is he funny? Is he edgy, responsible, a good kisser?

3. If a guy makes you hot, definitely keep dating him, but don't get too emotionally involved right away. Stand back and ask yourself, "What is making me want him so badly?"

4. Compare the men who make you hot with the men you consider nice guys. (Be prepared to LOL.) As a bonus, feel free to use the nice guys in your life to keep you occupied so that you're not too available for the "hottie" you really like. Sounds mean, but it's not. Let me explain: You don't have to do a man's "homework" for him. He should be able to win your heart, and if he can't, then he's not worthy of you. Nice guys won't learn to be naughty by your being nice to them; you're doing them a favor!

5. Finally, chances are that if he turns you on he's a "real guy." Let him know (without actually saying it!) that you understand his desire to be male. This "acceptance," if you will, will separate you from 90 percent of the female population. Meaning, if he's a little rowdy sometimes, if he's got a hobby—a motorcycle, for example—or a sport he "just has to spend time on," then embrace it, but let him know you won't play second fiddle all the time. This way, you're not there as filler in between his "guy time" and work. You are *part* of his guy time.

Q&A

Q: I've already dated Bad Boys, and now I want a nice guy. Do I do the same things you advise with any guy?

A: I don't believe you will never be attracted to a completely and totally "nice guy." However, that doesn't mean you want a Bad Boy, either. But by understanding Bad Boys, the man who *does* heat you up will be easier to deal with. So, yes, keep in mind the strategies and concepts you read in this book, even if the man you choose doesn't seem all that bad. Most women want a good man with an edge, and that, my friend, comes in many packages.

The fact that you're reading this Manual means that you are actively seeking information that will make you better able to understand guys, and therefore have more fun with the kind of man who gets you hot . . . but not so hot that he burns you. You're on your way! If you listen to the advice in *The Manual*, I promise you'll be able to handle the kitchen no matter how high the temperature.

Chapter 4

Do You Like Bad Boys?
A Quiz

Although you might still be denying it, there is no doubt that almost all women love some degree of Bad Boy. If you're saying to yourself, "Absolutely not. I want a nice guy who treats me sweetly," then fill out this questionnaire and find out how much "bad" you're really looking for in a man.

1. Who do you find the sexiest?
   a. Colin Farrell
   b. Leonardo DiCaprio
   c. Dave Matthews
   d. Homer Simpson

2. Who's the most appealing?
   a. A guy holding a guitar
   b. A guy holding a baby
   c. A guy walking a puppy

3. Who would you spend an entire day thinking about?
   a. A guy who calls you consistently
   b. A guy who's bought you flowers
   c. A guy who hasn't called you back
   d. A guy who was voted most likely to get arrested

4. What's the most important when it comes to a guy?
    a. He's rich.
    b. He's sexy.
    c. He drives a hot car.
    d. He's supermotivated on the job.

5. Do you like tattoos on guys?
    a. Yes
    b. No
    c. Some

6. The men you like tend to have
    a. A lot of male friends
    b. Mostly female friends
    c. An even mix
    d. Loner tendencies

7. What do you think looks best?
    a. An unshaven face (2+ days' growth)
    b. A clean-shaven face
    c. A beard
    d. A goatee or other facial art

8. What would be the most exciting to cruise around in?
    a. A Porsche along winding roads
    b. An SUV in the woods
    c. A motorcycle anywhere
    d. A minivan doing the speed limit

9. Which is the most important male trait?
    a. He's a great kisser.
    b. He's always on time.
    c. He puts the toilet seat down.
    d. He's got a great haircut.

10. The guy you prefer is most likely to listen to
    a. Classic rock
    b. Rap and techno
    c. Headbanger music
    d. Female artists

11. What's the sexiest?
    a. A guy who's good with a computer
    b. A guy who's good with a wrench
    c. A guy who's great in the kitchen
    d. A guy who's great at sports

12. Who's the most exciting?
    a. A musician
    b. A jock
    c. A suit
    d. A good friend

13. When it comes to how a guy dresses, what's hottest?
    a. Jeans and a T-shirt
    b. A shirt and tie
    c. All black
    d. Khakis and a polo shirt

14. Which body type do you like best?
    a. Ripped
    b. Athletic
    c. Huggable teddy bear
    d. Regular with a little fat

15. When it comes to animal attraction, what is a guy's most powerful weapon?
    a. The way he smells
    b. The way he smiles
    c. His eyes
    d. His shoulders

16. If you heard that the guy you liked had kissed another girl, you would
    a. Forget him
    b. Want him even more
    c. Be angry at the girl who kissed him
    d. Try to steal him away from her

17. What's the longest you would go without hearing from a guy before you called him to find out what's up?
    a. Two days
    b. Five business days
    c. A week
    d. Two moon cycles

18. Which is the biggest turnoff?
    a. He can't change a tire without calling for help.
    b. He asks what you would like to do on the date instead of having a plan of his own.
    c. He waits too long to try to kiss you.
    d. He looks at other girls when he's with you.

19. Would you go out with a guy with a bad reputation?
    a. Yes
    b. No
    c. Depends on how hot he is

20. Which type of dog best describes the kind of temperament you like in a guy?

   a. Golden retriever

   b. Rottweiler

   c. Mutt

   d. Chihuahua

21. Bonus Question: Do you like Bad Boys?

   a. Yes

   b. No

If you want to know just how good bad is to you, here's how to figure it out:

Below are the answers that would make you the ultimate lover of Bad Boys:

1a, 2a, 3d, 4b, 5a, 6b, 7a, 8c, 9a, 10a, 11b, 12a, 13a, 14b, 15b, 16b, 17b, 18a, 19a, 20c, and 21a.

Start off with a hundred points. For each "less than Bad" answer, deduct five points. For example: If you chose five "un–Bad Boy" answers, that would mean you lean 75 percent toward Bad Boys. If you chose eleven to fifteen "un–Bad Boy" answers, then you lean more toward "nice guys." And if you chose zero Bad Boy answers, I would check your pulse immediately.

Chapter 5

How Bad Boys Bring Out the Best in Women

So you like us.

Why is that a good thing? Bad Boys sure don't sound good, do they?

But you want to be around someone who brings out the best in you, and that often means a boy behaving badly. These types of men can get your blood boiling, and bring out the spirit in your body. Just like every woman has a spicy side, every man has a bit of the devil in him—and we like to use it.

This sometimes causes you to shriek at us in frustration. But letting these emotions out is a good thing. Guys rarely do this, and it's just one of the ways in which women can be more entertaining than men: You're funny, intelligent, sensitive, have a dirty sense of humor, and you talk about your "emotions." You're alive, and when you act like this, it makes *us* feel alive. We love feeling alive.

Think about it: Day-to-day living can become monotonous. We wake up and go through our days, and things get boring. I've always liked stirring things up a bit—which in turn stirs you up a bit. Which you love. Admit it . . .

The Three Ways Bad Boys Stir You Up

Letting a guy tap into your *zany side*—which your previous guy may have been either too lazy or too stupid to try—can be a blast for both of you. Unsure whether you're with a Bad Boy or not? This Bad Boy uses three tricks with female friends or girlfriends alike to keep things interesting. Here are my strategies—see if any of them looks familiar:

1. We Tell You You're Beautiful

- Every woman is unique in and of herself, and I pay extra-special attention to noticing every curve and every mannerism. For example, I rarely go for the obvious compliment. Instead, I praise a dimple, the color of her hair, her nose, or the cute way she walks.
- I compliment a woman on how beautiful she is in a way that is special to her. I went out with a girl whose lips curled into a snarl like Billy Idol's every time she laughed. She was very self-conscious of this, but I loved it and would scream, "More, more, more!" and kiss her every time she laughed—which of course made us both laugh harder, and I got to see more lip-snarling.
- I treat a woman special by the way in which I do things for and with her. I might do something totally unexpected, such as brush her hair while we're watching television, or buy her something to help her with work, or have her lie beside me and find shapes in the clouds. Albeit, most of the shapes I see involve something completely foul or dirty . . . but we have fun nonetheless.

A lot of men don't realize that the more beautiful a girl feels, the more easygoing she is. I love making women feel beautiful just for the sake of making them feel beautiful; it's an ego boost for me to have that power.

2. We Encourage Naughtiness

- I encourage the girl I'm with to open up about fantasies.
- I never judge her on what she's done in the past. I am serious about this. No matter the scenario, I cast no stones!
- I have fun with mild forms of talking dirty and playing games.
- I *never kiss and tell*. I'm private, and that's 90 percent of the fun—the secrets.

It's important for a woman to feel safe feeling naughty, and it's the guy's job to create that safe environment. Women are just as bad as we are, but society labels you when you express those thoughts. In the bedroom, you should feel safe and open. (See Chapter 44 for more.)

3. We Occasionally Fight

Have you ever had a guy seem to pick a fight with you on purpose, for no apparent reason? Early in a relationship, I will often intentionally press a woman's buttons to see what she's made of. You learn a lot about a person from how she behaves when she's angry. It's okay for couples to yell and scream on occasion. In fact, I want it. Remember the bit above about feeling *alive*? Passion and anger are right next to each other on the emotional scale.

I am, of course, not *promoting* violence, aggression, or unnecessary fighting. But I've come across many women who don't articulate the way they feel. They bottle it up until it all comes pouring out in a tirade. Just remember: you can't take back words, and you'd better be able to take it if you dish it out.

In the end, it all comes down to the fact that *passion*—yes, I mean beauty, naughtiness, and fights—makes both men and women feel really and truly alive. And encouraging this behavior is one of the major talents of Bad Boys.

Chapter 6

The Nurture of the Beast

We're not like you. We're boys. We're raised differently. Think of how often you were with other girls as a child, while the boys were nowhere in sight, off by themselves. Something happened in those early, gender-sequestering days. While you were brushing Malibu Barbie's hair, we were running expressionless Ken through the garbage disposal—and then avoiding Mom's wrath with an adorable grin, Ken's left leg in hand. Boys learn very early on that being bad feels right. And getting away without punishment? Even better.

What takes a little devil over the edge into Bad Boy adulthood? Rules. You can imagine how "creative" a boy might get at hiding his naughty deeds to avoid a stinging behind. A wink and a grin worked wonders on mothers, teachers, and sisters alike, so why wouldn't it work on romantic partners?

Whether throwing snowballs at cars, fighting in the school yard, or peeking into the girls' locker room, being bad feels *good*. Still does. Mothers, don't let your babies grow up to be cowboys? No. Don't let your babies grow up to be Bad Boys!

The true making of a Bad Boy begins with the opening of Pandora's box: the discovery of women. By the ripe old age of nine, I was already fascinated with my babysitter's chest, looking under the teacher's skirt, sneaking glances at *Playboy*, and longing for my first kiss. To me, this behavior was normal and, thankfully, unsupervised. By age ten, my fascination with the female form translated into talking my sixteen-year-old babysitter into flashing her chest in the garage. I was too young to know why I liked that, but I'd get to the bottom of it . . . and the top, and every other part, when I became an adult. Rebellious I was, and rebellious I would always be. Thus are the beginnings of the devil inside: an unquenchable thirst for understanding everything there is to know about girls.

I grew up living with my two sisters, my mom, and a little brother. Estrogen-o-rama. I admit that, at the time, I hated it. Of course, I now realize what important groundwork my household laid for my future exploits.

I quietly learned from the mistakes of boys who tried, and failed, to win dates with my sisters: they called too much, came on too fast, or tried to be "too nice." Not me. I wasn't going to be like those losers. I was going to get whom I wanted. But hold on. Believe it or not, I was shy—which is a problem if you're trying to meet girls. On top of being shy, I was also self-conscious about my bad skin, and the combination just didn't serve me. It took the wind out of my self-esteem, and self-esteem is something women like. (Special note: I'm not always confident. Over the years, though, I've learned that faking confidence during my insecure periods gets me through. Something to consider.)

As with most guys, college was when things shifted into high gear. I had sex for the first time. Girls, girls, girls, and more girls. There were all shapes and sizes. Dorm life is like a boy's lab, where I could carry out my mad scientific experiments to see what worked and what didn't to create the perfect get-'em-in-bed-quick elixir.

Something else happened at college: A lot of guys didn't want to be around me. They were competitive. I had thought we were all in the same pack. But, no. There were those who were successful with the ladies, and those who weren't. It seemed there was a price to pay for knowing so much about women. Oh well, I figured, I like girls and have no problem surrounding myself with them. Needless to say, most of my friends were women, and they still are today. Again, if you're around women all the time, you learn a lot about them. Knowledge is power, power to use for seduction.

By the time I got midway through my time at Emerson College, in Boston, the popular movement was for men to get in touch with their feminine side. What?! We have a *feminine side*? Is she hot? Not wanting to be misconstrued as a complete male chauvinist pig, I gave my feminine side a visit. This will forever be known as the Great Dry Spell. Women didn't like me when I was being "nice" and asking them about their feelings. They didn't respond to me when I was in touch with my feminine side. So I looked my feminine side in the eye, told her I loved her, and put her on a one-way bus out of town. (I haven't seen her since.) That was when I decided that if bad was what women wanted, bad was what they'd get. And, as I and all my peers have learned, *it works.*

Not all Bad Boys are brought up the same way, but most have had a similar experience, and every man with a fire burning inside knows what I'm talking about. Every woman who has ever been attracted to a man knows that unspoken quality that turns her on: some call it an edge, some call it a touch of the devil, some call it Bad Boy behavior, but whatever it's called, it's got to be there to ignite chemistry.

Life is a game to Bad Boys—that is, to those of us who possess full-body versions of Bad Boyness—and it always will be. The women we like play the game with us. And, quite frankly, the game, and we, are just not that complicated: We like women who are sexy, and we like to win. End of story.

If you listen, we'll tell you everything you need to know about how we feel about you, what we're doing, and what we plan to do next. Now let me teach you how to listen.

Inside the Male Mind: How He Sees You

Let me tell you a little secret about how to take advantage of how men think. *Bait us with your body, then keep us with your brains.* This is the way to keep a man. It's that simple. Looking good and dressing with the idea that you want to attract men gives a woman options. I'll elaborate: You've heard of "beer goggles," when a man sees a woman as hotter than she really is because he's drunk. Well, men have a kind of "lens" they see the female population through, even when they're sober. If you take advantage of what I've written in this book, men will begin to see *you* with twenty/twenty clarity. If not, you'll be a blur. The choice is yours. You have to be seen if you're ever going to be heard.

We care about what's between your ears, not just your legs. We don't want to spend our whole lives with airheads. But no matter how sensitive and smart we might be, we're initially attracted by your looks and sexiness. So what to do? Look good, and once you've got us circling like sharks on the high seas, it's time to talk some sense into us, and get our minds interested in the "rest" of the wonderfully intelligent you, from the neck up. But we initially need be attracted to your outside.

The women who understand and use the best aspects of their bodies are the ones who have the best choices in men! Thus, every part of a woman's body should be used to manipulate a man. Does that sound harsh? My goal is not to objectify you; it's simply to inspire you to become an object of desire. Peacocks have feathers to attract the opposite sex with, just like you have your appearance. You always need to pay attention to the message you are sending out. When you are trying to attract and keep potential mates, you *must* think about these things.

Chapter 7

Window Dressing

One female tendency will never make sense to me: that women dress to impress *other* women, especially single women. Why would a single woman dress with her friends or colleagues in mind? Is it because she doesn't want to be looked down upon by her peers? Is she showing off her excellent taste in clothes? Is she worried what other women will think of her?

Whatever the reason, this one habit alone could be killing your love life.

The number one way to significantly boost your chances of attracting Mr. Right is to think *sexy first, then style.* The looks that are stylish and cool are, most often, totally wasted on 99.9 percent of the male population. We could care less about your Manolo blah blah Blahniks or Jimmy Choo choo choos. Stick with Payless; we couldn't care less.

To get noticed, you need to dress in a way that guys can understand. Take a tip from us: When it comes to dressing, men think *comfortable and appealing to women,* usually in that order. A major concern is "Will girls think I'm cool in this?" We also assume that you like to know what our bodies look like, so we try wearing clothes that show our bodies' shape—or hide it, whichever is more flattering.

Some men might not admit it, but we love a hint of "trampy" in everything that women wear. (Notice I said a *hint.*) It's fun, and it's a turn-on. Look at the women on the covers of the bestselling men's magazines: the outfits (what little the women are wearing) are cheap. Men like a little cheap. (Again, a *little*.) Girls who wear a bit of sex appeal on their sleeve are not considered sluts by us guys; they're considered smart and dateable!

I know how ruthless women can be in judging one another. But remember, they're envious, and they don't care if you're home alone on a Friday night. So screw them and dress to kill . . . men. Men turn to look at a hint of sexiness a million times faster than at a hint of style. Once you have our attention, you've got options, but you *must* catch our attention. Overtly stylish women rarely grab our attention. We look at those girls as high maintenance, and on the rare occasion that we date one, we're only there to see how they look out of all that stuff.

The truth is that you can have both sex appeal and style. Find a combination that makes you feel stylish but that also stimulates our primitive male psyche. And then *wear it.* Those hot outfits are not to be kept in your closet. A rule of thumb: If you don't feel the tingle of raciness when you look in the mirror, then chances are you're missing it. In general it's better to lean toward naughty if you are trying to meet men.

Bottom line: Your girlfriends won't make you happy sitting by a fire or kissing you on the couch. Just get with it and dress the way nature intended: to appeal to the opposite sex!

Chapter 8

The Rest of the Closet

If you're really serious about meeting a man, then everything you do in the name of fashion, be it with your hair, your shoes, your lingerie, or your clothing, should take the male perspective into account.

I say "account" because no one wants to cater *only* to men, nor should they: if we had it our way, women would dress like cheerleaders or don tight jeans and flimsy tank tops all year long. Instead, you want to balance your sense of style with your understanding of what men notice.

Men Are No Different

I'll tell you a secret: Do you think I enjoy taking women's clothes preferences into account when I reach into my closet? Not really. Sometimes I want to be a complete slob. More than once I've wanted to shave my head and not have to deal with hair. And I'd be a lot richer if I didn't have to buy anything besides Levi's and black T-shirts. Hell, I wear the same waist size I did in high school, so why not just keep clothes until they're moth-eaten and falling off my body? Because if I want to be attractive to women, I have to think about what they like, whether I like it or not. I have to stay in shape, brush my teeth, and execute at least a vague sense of fashion. In their eyes, I have to look as attractive on the outside as I am on the inside.

Attention to vanity will seem shallow at times, but in the game of love, it's very important. Most people I see are lazy in this department. And, not surprisingly, these are the same people who complain, saying things such as "People are so superficial," "I want him to love me for what's *inside*," or "I hate the gym." Well, no one is telling you that you can't dress as you choose. But when you put those constraints on yourself, *you're limiting the number of men who will find you attractive.* In the end, meeting the right person is a numbers game, and part of getting those numbers rolling is how you dress.

Here's how to attract men's eyes.

A Woman's Closet, Designed by Men

Lingerie

Lingerie can be inexpensive, but it can't be the kind that comes in a package of three (white, pink, and blue). Nor can it be the "granny" kind with a waist that reaches up to your rib cage and that hangs like a diaper. Lingerie is one garment that you should find as sexy as he does. And it benefits you, too. Women have told me that when they wear nice underwear, even though no one may see it, they will actually walk and talk differently, just knowing they have a little sexy secret. If lingerie can do that to a woman—and we already know how it affects men—then don't you think you should go out and get yourself some? You have tons of choices, and when it comes to lingerie, men like just about anything.

Shoes

Again, *we don't care.* We know you like them. We don't understand why you like them. All we know is that many of you have closets full of them, and we've figured out that since you spend so much time and money on them, we can compliment them to flatter you. That's about it.

Most likely, if a guy tells you what nice shoes you have, he's either gay or "working you." My friend Mari recently told me that a guy came up to her in the airport and complimented her on new shoes. She's so sweet that she thought he meant it. I'm not saying that they're not nice shoes. But have you ever heard a man say, "Well, the thing that caught my eye was Shirley's shoes. I love those pumps, and when I saw them I knew she was the woman for me"? I don't know a single male who would say, "Dude, this chick had the hottest shoes on last night. Damn, I should've gotten her number." It doesn't happen. Shoe flattery is for one purpose only: flattery. Have I made my point?

There *is* one style of shoes that men notice, and that's high heels. But heels are more about what a girl looks like in them than about the shoes themselves. Heels make feet and legs look sexy. The classic example is a girl wearing high heels in a bikini. Cheesy, and not particularly functional in the sands of Miami and L.A., but men notice for sure.

Hair

Hair, on the other hand, is, sigh, one of the sexiest things about a woman. Hair grabs us and doesn't let us go. Think octopus tentacles. Your style, color, and texture are no matter. Your hair only needs to have a clean, tousled, just-out-of-bed look. My opinion is that most women look sexier with longer hair than shorter. Men like long, sexy hair largely because we don't have it. Plus, very few women can get away with that short boyish look. Next time you're out in public, watch how men look at women with long hair versus short.

On a related note, hair salons suck. I can't believe what they've done to some of your mops. They're not just ruining your hair; they're wrecking your love life. With the Internet and a gazillion fashion magazines at your fingertips, you've got plenty of references. Please think sexy and spend the time and money to get the right do. When in doubt, turn to whichever celebrity women are getting the most attention for being sexy, and copy them. Messy sexy is what you should be after: think Sheryl Crow, Jessica Alba, Jane Seymour, and Reese Witherspoon.

A few more tips: Don't color your hair based on the swatches you picked up at the paint store. Other styles to avoid include bad bangs, mullets, and that "business in the front/party in the back" look. And stop cutting your hair short as you age—there's no need to.

Dresses

Every woman wears a dress differently. The only hard-and-fast rule is to *pick a dress that accentuates your best body parts.* Whether you have a gorgeous back, incredible thighs, or lovely collarbones, stock up on designs that not only fit but also highlight those attributes.

Your shape and height determine much of what you'll look good in, but here are some general rules of thumb:

Shorter Girls

- Wear heels. Heels create the illusion of longer legs. And as I've said, they're sexy!

- Buy a dress that vaguely clings, while still allowing your bum to move freely. Check out the red carpet "best dressed" lists for examples.

- Loose cotton dresses are best if you have some pounds to shed. They give us a hint of your bum and legs without a solid picture. We have vivid imaginations and we fantasize you better-looking, not worse. (We're on your side here. Just give us something to work with!)

Taller Girls

- Stand up straight, shoulders back, chest high.

- Wear longer dresses that hug your legs a bit. You want a fitted design.

- Pick either heels or flats, depending on how tall you want to appear.

- Make sure that at least 60 percent of your skin is covered by the dress. You have a lot of skin, and a little goes a long way.

- As with shorter girls, loose-fitting, sheer cotton dresses that cling a little are great for those of you carrying a bit of extra weight.

Tops and Bottoms

This is fairly straightforward: You need to have tops and bottoms in your closet that, you have no doubt, are "man killers." Call it your "good luck resisting me" section. This is the part of the closet that houses the cleavage cuts, the tighty tops, and the bootylicious jeans. Feel free to mix and match from the more "domestic" side of your closet, but never forget: It's a jungle out there, and sometimes it pays to get a little wild if you want to survive!

Glasses

Glasses are hot! Hands down. Just make sure you pick a great style that flatters your face and keep the lenses free of eyelashes and fingerprints. I love chicks in glasses.

Chapter 9

Halloween Tricks

L et's talk about the "Halloween Phenomenon." Each October, women across the country simultaneously dress up in every conceivable version of sexy: nurses, superheroes, waitresses, flight attendants, cheerleaders, and French maids. I'm far from the first to notice this. For men, this is our favorite holiday. Long after you've put away the pumpkin and begun hanging tinsel, men are still reliving their trick-or-treat fantasies.

If you have any interest in attracting men in day-to-day life, then you can learn a lot from this holiday. Men love women in sexy costumes. I know, I know: It's not feminist-friendly to suggest that you don a Little Red Riding Hood cape. That's not where I'm going. And I know that many of you care what other women think of you, and wouldn't be caught dead in those Dorothy pigtails on any other day. I'm not going there, either. Instead, I am going to show you how you can attract the same male attention the other 364 days of the year by using the same festive dress all year long without looking like a slut.

For those of you who don't understand why women pull out all the stops on Halloween costumes, I'll explain it briefly: Because they can. This is the one day of the year—New Year's Eve runs a close second—when women can feel free to dress risqué without being ridiculed by their peers. It's an annual "get out of ho jail free" card. It's fun. And not surprisingly. I can't tell you how often women gush to me about all the guys who hit on them while they were dressed as Snow White.

Please don't kid yourself into thinking that the guy you're after isn't into this stuff. All men like hints of costume. If your guy likes women, he'll notice, and find you not only special and sexy, but also a lot of fun. As men scan the streets, the malls, and the workplace, we often classify women into "types." And at no other time of year are types more defined than on Halloween. Bash us you may, but I'm telling it to you straight: when it comes to women, men love *simple* and *easy to define.*

The trick to keeping your Halloween treats working for you all year is to incorporate a bit of your costume's "essence" into your everyday wardrobe. Here's how:

1. Take a look at yourself in the mirror and figure out what costume stereotype you might easily fit into. Who do you want to be for Halloween? The naughty nurse? The dominatrix? The schoolteacher? Pick something sexy.

2. Find out the one piece that is the essence of that costume and discreetly incorporate it into your everyday wardrobe. Examples include: bows, braids, pigtails, and the disheveled secretary look (you know, like you just got it on at your desk). Pay attention to details like cute glasses, jewelry, hairstyles, and shoes. Sometimes it can be something only you know you're wearing. Oh, and black is always good, especially in thigh-high boots or a button-up silk shirt.

3. Show off one aspect of your body. Men's eyes usually attach themselves to one or two body parts, so pick one part and bet it all. Sometimes a woman will try to accentuate her whole body, yet no one thing on her looks particularly good. Stick with one thing. Wear your hair a certain way, add something black, reveal a little more cleavage than normal, wear a tight skirt, or try on some glasses. The trick is to keep trying things until you see what gets the most attention.

Unsure of which costumes work for you? Halloween is like a huge lab experiment that never fails! Be creative this year and pay close attention to your effect on men. Try out different outfits at the costume and theme parties that pop up on your calendar. Once you've nailed down your look, take advantage of its sexy essence all year.

Keep pushing the envelope. Remember, the point here is not a perfectly accurate costume. When someone says, "Hey, you look just like Dorothy!" you know it's time to head back over the rainbow. When four people ask you for your number, you know you're on the money.

Chapter 10

Bum's the Word

We love your bum! We love your round bum, your little bum, your big bum, your flat bum, your cute bum. Most of the men I know will eventually tire of a nice chest, but they will rarely wear out a nice bum . . . so to speak. For every type of bum, there's a man.

I'm here to tell you that there is power in your bum and you're not using it—probably because you're too self-conscious. I see you outside clothing store dressing rooms: The first thing you do when trying something on is turn around, look over your shoulder, and see if your ass looks good. Always! So put those instincts to use in your daily life. Here's how to make your best natural asset work for you.

Flattering the Bum

It's too bad that you don't have eyes in the back of your head. If you did, you would realize how often your bum is looked at. Men are constantly gazing at bums, and yours is no exception. Here's what you can do to get the most bang from your bum.

1. Don't wear outfits that don't flatter your style of bum. In other words, work within the framework of the shape you were born with. *Accentuate* no matter what.

2. Wear heels. (I know. Heels again? But it's a good tip.)

3. Keep your shoulders back and chest high. Walk casually but consciously, straight and tall. Then mildly tighten your bum while walking. It looks good.

4. Try not to "march" or walk like a guy. (You know what I mean.) Use whatever feminine stride works for you.

Bum-Flattering Clothing

I want your bum to look good. In order for that to happen, you have to wear clothes that at least vaguely hug it. I am not suggesting you wear booty-squeezing pants at work. But any businessman will tell you that he appreciates a co-worker in a well-tailored pair of pants. And a good pair of jeans, a fitted skirt, or tight sweat pants are a bum's best friend. Baggy pants are to be avoided. Pay attention to the cuts of all pants and skirts, and make sure you're getting the most out of your rear view.

Panty Lines

Every time I see a television ad telling women how to get rid of panty lines, my heart sinks. That would be unfortunate, because panty lines do two things for men:

1. Tell us what kind of undies you have on.
2. Give us a good idea of what your bum looks like without clothes on.

We enjoy a little bit of panty line, perhaps because your panties are so dramatically different from ours. Think about it. Men have written songs about women's underwear! No one writes songs about men's. Men's underwear is ugly and boring and comes in only three styles and about five colors. But you have so many mysterious options, and each day we want to know which one you've chosen!

I know, I know, this is another piece of advice that goes against what your girlfriends suggest. Other women do not appreciate panty lines. But remember whose attention you're trying to attract.

We also enjoy over-the-top panties—the sort that literally hang out of the top of your low-cut jeans and skirts, or that peek out when you lean over for a second. Even the slightest glimpse of a piece of a panty gets us thinking.

Bum Maintenance

The classically perfect bum is round and fairly firm. Most everyone, men and women alike, agree on this. But, in truth, men like all sorts of bums. What we don't like is a lazy bum. A lazy bum is one that doesn't get much exercise and therefore looks neglected and shapeless. You see, a bum's shape can vary, but it has to have a shape. Any shape. Don't worry if your bum isn't classic. Your goal is to make it the best bum in its class.

Bum exercises can be done just about anywhere, so there's no excuse. The simple "invisible clench" move works wonders: an easy matter of tightening your glut muscles while reading or at work. I see so many of you squandering this precious backside resource. Get to it and use it!

Chapter 11

Cleavage, and Other Reasons to Wear a Shirt Well

When I lived in Australia, I stayed in a little hotel with a café on the ground floor. I started each morning downstairs, ordering coffee and a bite to eat. But, more important, I was there to be waited on by Natasha. Oh my God! Natasha had the best chest I had ever seen. I'm sure there are other women with just as wonderful breasts, but Natasha had a very nonchalant way of carrying hers: white tank top and no bra. I was dead. I couldn't even talk to her. I could barely even look at her. And I still remember her ten years later.

You see, men are prone to a state known as "tit dizziness." It comes on often, many times a day, and puts us in a mild stupor, completely distracted from the tasks at hand. A number of sights can induce this affliction. Examples include:

- buttons pulling on a blouse;
- a hint of cleavage;
- a top hugging the outline of a woman's breast; and
- visible bra straps.

It's amazing that our eyes don't turn into pinwheels because, for lack of a better description, when we see breasts we're absolutely hypnotized. While under the mysterious spell of the breast, men have wrecked cars and fallen down stairs. The truth is, we can't help it. For us, not looking is not natural. Looking at your chest is an involuntary response so deeply rooted that we must make a concerted effort *not to look.* In today's society, when we're with a woman, checking out another woman just lacks class, so we do it subtly. But know this: if you're out with your man and you see an attractive woman walk by, chances are he has noticed before you and is showing great restraint by not staring.

> Note: If your man spontaneously hugs you in public, look behind you. Sometimes there's a girl he wanted to check out. I've done it, and I'm not alone.

Despite the power of tit dizziness—you can attract a wide variety of men in bars and clubs, for example, not to mention the lawyer who lives next door—single women everywhere fail to use what they have to their advantage. I know. You prefer to dress "appropriately," or maybe you feel that your breasts aren't your best feature. But every rack is beautiful, and there's nothing that a good bra can't fix. Remember, you're creating the *image* of breasts.

In the jungle that is relationships, you need to utilize every weapon in order to win. Making us tit dizzy is such a weapon. When men see a woman's chest in just the right way, something chemical happens, and we automatically pay attention. It's a primitive response.

There's a right way and a wrong way to hypnotize us. The idea is to *tease,* not expose yourself. In fact, you can even tease effectively while in winter gear or dressed for work. Here are some suggestions:

How to Clothe Your Chest

Small Breasts (size A to small B)

Look at the way small-chested models dress—they've got it down:

- in tank tops;
- in tight-fitting T-shirts;

- braless in a way that lets us know you're braless—in a low-back top, for example; and
- revealing an outline of nipple through a white T-shirt or on a cold day.

Medium Breasts (size B to small C)

- in push-up bras with the cleavage exposed;
- in a tight sweater over a push-up bra—or no bra, if they're perky (perfect cold-weather strategy);
- in a blouse that's one size too small (this creates pulling buttons, which drives men absolutely nuts; we can't handle it); and
- in an untucked tight T-shirt (the bit of midriff at the bottom makes it look like your chest is so pert it's elevating the shirt; always works).

Big Chest (full C to double-D)

- Vary your cleavage depending on the situation. You don't want to look like you're trying too hard. Feel free to flaunt it when you're on the beach or in Vegas.
- Tone it down a little if they're big. Wear clothes that make you look busty but not overwhelming. The idea is to tease. Hint: black tops minimize your girls, while loose tops camouflage them.
- Mix it up. Wear something that is busty one day and conservative the next. This makes us pay attention, creates in us a desire to know more, and gets us wondering whether they're big or huge.

Not sure how well an outfit is working? Look at the eyes of the men you pass during your daily activities. If they're checking you out, you've done a good job.

You can use our fascination with your chest as a sort of "carrot on a stick" and lead us around. Once we tire of being led, though, we'll snap out of it, so use it early on and use it wisely. Older men tend to have built up an immunity to such tactics, while college guys won't know what hit 'em. At every age, the better your "chest display," the longer that power will remain. You want to keep men distracted while you pull them in, so much so that they won't even notice your reasonable relationship demands. Try asking your man to take you to the ballet while wearing a deliciously revealing tank top. You'll have tickets for that night.

Q&A

Q: I'm a lawyer. I spent many years earning my degree and the respect of my peers, and I'm not about to go flashing my cleavage to win a man. Is there another way?

A: Yeah, there's another way: get a mail-order bride catalogue and see if there are any men who look good. No, there is no other way. Men are visual creatures, whether or not you have a JD. Get over yourself and start being unapologetically sexy.

Girls who know how to work it can use their bodies as powerful negotiators. How powerful? A minor shirt readjustment can make your man forget his own thoughts. I once dated a woman who would humorously strip down to her bra every time we were having a tiff. I couldn't even remember what I was mad about!

Now that you know these secrets, use your chest effectively. Walking around in unflattering clothes that are about as exciting as grocery coupons won't help attract men. Ladies, men are visual creatures, and your chest is part of your visual allure. Use it. Why not "stack" the deck in your favor?

Chapter 12

Get a Leg Up

In the game of attracting men, putting on a skirt or shorts once in a while is the equivalent of stealing a base. It's the easiest way to advance. An old song by the band ZZ Top put it best: "She's got legs and she knows how to use 'em."

Legs are great and powerful. The mere act of a woman crossing her legs can drive a guy wild. Legs in short skirts or shorts? Even better. When I say *short*, I mean anything above the knee. If you're tall, half of your leg could conceivably be covered. Of course, as a general rule, the shorter the skirt or shorts, the greater the response you'll get from men. Long live the miniskirt!

Imagine what you can do with your legs when you really know how to take advantage of them. Think of wearing a skirt or shorts as the difference between using a plastic worm versus live bait when fishing. Skirts and shorts are like live bait for men, because your bum and your legs appear *au naturel*. What kind of skirt or shorts to wear? Go by the fashion trends of the time. Whatever the current craze, exposed legs will never go out of style!

Skirting Around

Skirts and dresses serve three main purposes in the eyes of men, none of which has to do with style:

1. They show off your legs.

2. They allow us to see your bum moving without the restraint of pants. This is more natural and allows more movement, all of which adds up to more attraction.

3. They let us know that there isn't anything in front of "home base." That's a turn-on.

Skirts look best if they are fitted but not too tight. "Too tight" deforms the shape of your bum and impedes your walking, neither of which is attractive. When we see a woman wearing a skirt that's too tight, we worry she's going to fall down . . . which is not sexy. Women regularly make this mistake. If you have a little extra "junk in the trunk," then give that trunk some breathing room. My friend Kate puts it this way: "When I see girls in skirts or jeans that are too small, it's like they're trying to put ten pounds of rice in a five-pound sack—not a good look." Instead, you want your skirt just tight enough to outline your figure. It should neither suffocate you nor be so loose that you look sloppy.

It's also worth mentioning that the long, flowing skirts that regularly come into style are often lost on men. We can't see your bum or your legs. Your girlfriends may think you look great, but as far as we're concerned, you might as well be wearing a sack.

> Note: One of the hottest things a woman can do in a skirt is arch her back as she pushes luggage into the overhead compartment on a plane. Next time you fly and see a guy, why not try it?

Shorting It

A good pair of denim cut-off shorts on a hot summer day can be more attractive than your best clubbing outfit. We love your legs, and shorts create an ideal situation for everyone: you are comfortable and happy, and we can see your legs. When good weather comes around, don't forget this!

Bottom line: legs can be used to walk out on a man—why not use them to encourage a man to walk in?

Chapter 13

Body Beautiful: Makeup, Don't Break Up

Let's begin with an important tip: Never wash your face with soap. Even if you're a coal miner's daughter, you should rinse with warm water and moisturize. If you've applied something waterproof or stubborn, use makeup remover—or, for light makeup, an inexpensive moisturizer—and wipe it off with cotton pads. That's it. No soap, no mild cleanser. I modeled for twenty years, and this is what the smarter models do. (Yes, you can use the words *smart* and *model* in the same sentence.) By not stripping your skin with soap, you'll look young forever, assuming you don't smoke or tan too much. I know. Now you're thinking, "Who the hell is this guy? I thought I was reading a book on relationships!" Well, your beauty routine has a lot to do with your long- and short-term success in relationships.

Makeup and Men

Most of the men I know don't like too much makeup, preferring instead a simple, natural, and well-groomed look. After all, loads of makeup isn't fun in the bedroom; the sheets shouldn't look like the circus has just left town.

Men also don't like it when women spend a long time on their makeup routines. We get annoyed that you're hogging the bathroom, and impatient when we want to leave now and you need forty more minutes. Too much primp time is also risky because spending ample time on something so shallow can give your man the impression that your priorities are warped.

Below is a laundry list of cosmetic-related things that most guys like and don't like and why.

• Lipstick: We hate the taste of lipstick. Natural colors are best; we don't want to feel like we're making out with a doll.

• Thick makeup: Anything that rubs off on our clothes is disgusting.

• Botox: Eventually it makes you look like a freak.

• Lip injections: You look like you have two night crawlers on your face. Not a good look unless you're fishing. Thin lips *can* be sexy.

• Hair color: Absolutely. Choose whatever color or highlights you like. We love them all . . . except for old-lady purple.

• Perfume: A little goes a long way. Find a signature scent, and then spice it up a couple times a week.

• Breast enhancement: If you have a nice shape to your breasts (and that includes all sizes), then, *no*, you probably can't improve on what you've got. However, if you hate the size and shape of your chest (get a second opinion), feel you've lost your chest in the process of having children, or think that the rest of your body is "perkier" than your chest, then it's worth considering. Just don't get them too big, and have them done well.

• Tanning: A tan with or without tan lines is always good. We prefer tan lines—at least on your bottom—as sometimes girls without these lines tend to look a little cheap. But we know that too much tanning is horrible for your skin, and we like peaches-and-cream complexions, too.

• Face-lift: Sorry, but it looks horrible. See Hollywood red carpet arrivals for details.

- Liposuction: You're just putting a Band-Aid on a big fat problem.

- Manicure and pedicure: Go for it. An easy way to look well groomed.

The point here is that makeup and other body treatments can lightly augment your looks, but you *do not* want to "paint on your face." You all know that female friend who's not classically gorgeous yet has men at her beck and call? It's not because she looks like a Barbie. It's because she's naturally happy and comfortable with her body, and that projects through her face. Makeup can enhance your natural features, but it shouldn't be your calling card!

The Trick to an Easy Routine

When you're seeing a new guy, go to the first few dates in low-key makeup. It's best that he see the real you early on, with as little makeup help as possible. Let him fall for the sexiest natural version of you. Otherwise, if you doll yourself up the first four times he sees you (think clown makeup), you'll have to keep that up for the remainder of the relationship. Your natural look is easy for you to maintain, and the added bonus is that when you get all glammed up for a party or wedding, he'll think you're a totally new girl. We love that!

The moral to the story is that you should look the way you want to be treated. How you look is intricately connected to your sense of self. The more unnatural you are, the more we tend to objectify you. If you look like plastic, we may treat you that way, because that's the signal you're sending. Going natural is not the ticket to the sloppy train, but if you're naturally well-groomed, we'll pick up on that and respond by treating you like you look: great.

Chapter 14

The Tomboy: You Don't Have to Dress Up to Get Down

Although each man has his own opinion of what's "natural" and desirable, most men agree that simple beauty is better than the kind that requires high maintenance. We like girls in T-shirts. But what exactly is *too natural*? Too natural is a woman who demonstrates more male characteristics than female, namely burping all the time, swearing like a truck driver, or not showering. But tomboys can be completely, utterly, mind-bogglingly sexy. You'd be surprised at how many women do this well. Here's an explanation of how to ditch the heels and play up your tomboy appeal.

Why Men Love Tomboys

Jeans, a T-shirt, and a ponytail are among many men's favorite looks on a woman, regardless of her age. A guy's girl who can hang with us yet still look feminine? That's a combination made in heaven. We love it when a woman can be with the guys and isn't all prissy, especially when it comes to being active and getting outside. But we also like that she remains a lady.

This is a fine line to walk. Feel free to spit if you're on a run with us, or burp over a beer for a laugh, but if you naturally lean toward "tomboyishness," then you need to tone it down or you risk going overboard and becoming "one of the boys." You know that friend of yours who complains that she's always the *friend* of the guys she likes? She's one of the boys. And they love her, just not in the way she wants. Remember from the get-go: *you want to be the girlfriend, not the friend.* You are cute and tomboyish, but not a guy.

When it comes to socializing with men, the more "girly" you are, the more you can get away with in terms of acting "tomboyish." Anything that is against type is sexy and funny to us.

Mixing Up the Wardrobe

We like you in the tomboy style because it makes us feel like we're with a friend. Not a pal, but a friend who sort of likes us. A sexy friend who looks good in everything, whether it's a cocktail dress or a pair of work boots. The more looks you can pull off, the more interesting you'll appear. Tomboy looks work best when mixed with other styles, such as a T-shirt, jeans, boots, and a string of hippie beads, or shorts, a T-shirt, and high heels. For tomboy-style ideas, check out a women's surfing or outdoor magazine.

Boys, Tomboys, and Booze

The only reason we want to see you drunk is because we know it will be easy to have sex with you. *Do not get drunk in front of men.* It's dangerous, stupid, and unattractive, yet women across America seem to think it's a good idea. I talk about alcohol and dating in other sections of this Manual, but I'm belaboring the point here for a very important reason: Boys like to drink a lot and get rowdy, and if you're hanging with that crowd, you can get swept up in the moment. Going drink for drink with the guys is a bad idea. Tipsy is okay, but drunk is dumb. Just think of all your friends drunk. How often is their drunkenness flattering to them? Rarely, if ever. It's the same with you.

Chapter 15

Things Are Getting Hairy

There's a difference between *tomboy* and *oh boy*. I've spent a lot of time in rural Vermont, and I have seen plenty of women use the excuse that they're nonconformists for not shaving their legs, bikini area, and/or armpits. Even though many of these women get away with it (only because there are far more men than women in these rural areas), you should know that for better or worse, a lot of men find it disgusting. Right now shaving is very big in popular culture, and it's become what men expect, so you don't have much of a choice.

Bikini Beauty

Your bikini area is not the place to practice going *au naturel*. Take care of that area; consider it your Garden of Eden, and don't forget to weed it! Think Canada and other jungle-free regions, not the Amazon.

If you prefer to leave a "little grass" on the playing field, then get creative from time to time with the shape. There's even a product called Betty that's a color dye for the hair down there; shocking pink will make him stop and think. The point is to keep him guessing.

Part of what we like about women is that they're different from us, and their softness and lack of body hair is part of that.

A Note to the Guys

Ladies, show your men these paragraphs.

Dating is a two-way street: You guys should be conscious of keeping groomed, trimming what needs to be trimmed, and keeping clean. Women don't want to date a gorilla, either.

If you resisted the metrosexual era, have never gotten a manicure, and don't have more shoes than your woman, congratulations, you're still a guy. However, you shouldn't resist pulling out the weed whacker and trimming around the tree. It is not gay to trim around your "johnson," keep your chest hair to cashmere length, and stop the nose hair from getting in the way when you eat.

Note: The last thing men want is for a monkey to swing out on a vine from your jungle down under. That monkey won't be getting a banana.

Chapter 16

Shape Up, Shape Out

We all wear our most obvious weaknesses on our sleeves: our weight, skin health, and body posture. Together they tell people whether we're happy or sad, meticulous or lazy, whether we take good or poor care of ourselves, and whether we have a weakness for food or a lack of discipline for exercise. Because your body is the first thing that men (and everyone else) sees, you want it to be a reflection of your strengths, not your weaknesses.

You already know the many social, physical, and emotional reasons to stay in shape, so I won't preach them here. Instead, I'll talk about exercise, diet, sex, and love. What do these things have in common? They're all intertwined. How much you love yourself, your personal comfort level in the bedroom, and your feelings about your life and relationship are all intermingled with your diet and exercise habits.

Women have it hard. You've got the media banging down your door on all four topics, telling you that you're too fat or too skinny, suggesting a new diet or sex trick. It's overload. But what to do? You still want to look good for your current man, so you start exercising vigorously. You join a gym. You're going to be in shape! And hot! . . . and then you stop going to the gym. As any girl who's tried this plan knows, exercising for others doesn't work. It's difficult to be inspired to maintain a healthy regimen for a man who isn't even in your life, or for one who is there but isn't worth it. So, now what?

The key is to jump off the treadmill of perfection for other people. You should be exercising *for you*, doing activities that you enjoy and that are good for your body, all for your own enjoyment. You're enjoying how your body feels when you treat it well. These activities have nothing to do with men, sex appeal, or anything else. Start to think of healthy living as part of *your* life. Your exercise regimen is all about *you*. Even if you don't like yourself right now, take the first step onto a path of self-care and good relationships. It's as easy as a short walk or jog.

How Fitness Affects Your Love Life

There is no nice way of saying this: the better you look, the greater the number of men who will find you attractive. The same is true for men, but as you probably already know, men are slightly more shallow and less forgiving when it comes to looks. As I'll repeat over and over again, men are visual creatures! So you need to look good.

And again, the more men you attract, the more choices you'll have. By staying in shape, you'll give yourself the greatest chance of meeting that special someone you have chemistry with, of getting into that great relationship that doesn't make you "settle." In gym class, I was always the last kid picked, and it's no fun. You don't want to be the "last girl picked." And the way to prevent that is to keep in shape.

The good news is that any in-shape, well-groomed body can be attractive to hordes of men. Yes, it takes work and, yes, it takes commitment, but the rewards far outweigh the effort. Stop saying, "I want someone to like me for who I am inside." Most of the women

Note: Being liked for who you are on the inside is important, but you could be the best car on the lot, and if you're not a little shiny on the outside, a potential buyer will never check under your hood and take you for a spin.

I've met who say that they want to be loved for who they are inside are using this as an excuse not to get off their asses and take care of themselves.

It's a vicious circle. If you don't feel good about yourself, you don't do good things for yourself, and so on. Break the cycle! Look good, feel good, do good.

A Word on Being Too Thin

In most major cities, the "in" look is extreme thinness. *Men actually don't like this.* The next time you're in a crowd, pick out the bodies that you would like to hug. Who wants to hug a pile of bones? Not us! Thin is fine, but unnaturally skinny is pointless. Women who have starved themselves to perfection are actually advertising their vanity and dependence on men. Your female friends may be impressed by your lack of body fat, but we're not. We like women who are firm, in shape, and happy. Curves and a little "roundness" are wonderful!

The Bonuses of Being in Shape

Staying in shape has residual effects far beyond finding Mr. Right. From better jobs to looking younger to feeling more energetic to performing better at home and in the office, nothing gives you more bang for your buck than staying in shape. Exercise improves your quality of life. You will literally find yourself winning at everything!

Chapter 17

Confidence Is Sexy!

But sexiness is not primarily about looks. We all know a woman who is somehow incredibly sexy yet, objectively speaking, not all that attractive. That's because sexiness is all about how you carry yourself, how you enter a room.

There are plenty of physically attractive people who lack sexiness, and plenty of average-looking people who drip sex appeal. Think about the actors and actresses on the red carpet and how many times you've said to yourself, "He/she is actually quite normal-looking and yet so hot!" It's all in the way they carry themselves, and that special gleam in their eye.

You may think I'm an egomaniac for telling you this, but I'll risk it: when I walk into a public place and I'm looking to send out the "I'm a catch" vibe to women, I actively say things to myself such as "Let's see, which one of you do I want?" and "You should be so lucky to be with me," and "I can have any one of you!"

Do I really believe that? No. Sometimes I feel ugly and would rather go home and get in bed. But I walk, think, and act as if my "I'm too sexy for this place" attitude were true. Why? Because *your inner monologue is more visible than you think.* Tell yourself that you're worth a billion dollars and are the best catch in the room, and suddenly men will perceive you as such.

Don't puff up your chest and strut around. Simply walk calmly and casually and *think it.* Men like confident women, and that attraction can be more about the confidence a person carries than about her striking good looks.

You Are What You Think

When you walk into a room, focus your mind on something really sexy, really confident, and really naughty. This is yet another reason to don nice lingerie and get a fresh pedicure, even if no one will see them—feeling confident is much easier if you're dressed for succsex.

Topics to think about include:

- things you find romantic (dinner for two, walks on the beach, anything);
- a fantasy about the guy across the room—let your mind drift; or
- cut to the chase and just think about sex.

Have fun with this. Strangers have no idea what your strengths or weaknesses are, so if you're thinking strong and sexy thoughts, you will be perceived as strong and sexy. Even if you are at work, which is not usually conducive to this type of thought, try it out! The best part? Other women won't be able to pick up on your mindset, but the boys will.

Body Stance

Have you ever noticed how you walk when you're happy versus when you're sad? Have you ever perceived other people's feelings by the way they're standing? You know you have. Check out these three keys to sexy body language:

1. Great posture: Stand up straight and relax your shoulders and facial muscles.

2. Slow walk: Move a touch slower than normal.

3. Body awareness: Feel what your body's doing as it moves. Pay attention to your hip flexors and neck.

Try it—even if you have to fake it. It works.

What Not to Do

These are all major turnoffs, antithetical to sexiness:

- slouching;
- shifty eyes and/or lack of eye contact;
- an uptight stance or rigid gait;
- stressed-out behavior; an upset, annoyed, or bothered facial expression; and
- any wallflower behavior, such as leaning against a wall or avoiding the crowd.

The Eyes Have It

Practice holding someone's gaze a little longer than you normally would. Don't freak someone out and stare them down, but if you're on a date, you can hold the eye contact even longer. You don't have to bat your eyes or try to be sexy. Just hold a gentle gaze and think of something naughty, even if your conquest is telling you about his toolbox. You'll show him how to screw! (Kidding.) After sitting with you a while, he may become agitated by your quiet confidence . . . in a good way. He may even ask you what you are thinking—but he probably won't, for fear that he's wrong. If he does ask, your response should always be, "Oh, I'm just listening to you and thinking about what you're saying."

Perception is often greater than reality, and now it's time to use it to your advantage.

Chapter 18

Porn Explained

YYou're probably not interested in pornography. A lot of men, however, are.

Porn has been here for a very long time. (See cave drawings.) The good news is that most of us don't desire to date porn stars. We like normal women, like you. But men are visually oriented creatures, and the Internet and magazines are where we do our "window browsing." By looking at pictures, we decide what we like, what we don't like, and who's in our league.

When a man looks at porn, his inner dialogue might go something like this:

> *Oh, those are great.*
> *Wow, I've never seen that before.*
> *Pigtails! My favorite!*
> *Eeeww. No. Is that Paris Hilton?*

Objectifying? Yes. Degrading? Unfortunately, quite often. Yet all the women in professional porn (I use the term *professional* loosely) are willing to get naked and do the things we fantasize about. It's a fact of life.

Not all things porno are attractive. Many are quite sick, and any man's fascination with porn should only be a hobby. My intention is not to gross you out, but rather to enlighten you as to why we look at dirty pictures, and explain how you can use our habit to your advantage. Most guys won't tell you this stuff, but the more information you have, the better off you'll be. So let's address the tamer content one might find and why men like to look at it.

Want to know a secret? If we didn't think it would freak you out, men would stare at you and study your anatomy for hours on end. We're fascinated by your curves and shapes. We're always trying to sneak a peek when a woman is naked. But imagine if we hit the floodlights in the bedroom and said, "Okay, let's take a look. Hmmm. This is amazing! This little mark right there, it's so interesting!"

We can't stare at you, taking it all in; you'd think we were crazy. This leaves our interest unquenched. Hence, the need for porn. With porn, we can stare and examine until we get bored. Sometimes we look at porn for the obvious reasons, and sometimes we look at it the same way you would shop from a clothes catalogue. Each man has physical likes and dislikes, and the "porn catalogue" is how we decide which is which.

What This Means for You

Sadly, men do compare you to the women we see online and in magazines, the same way you compare yourself to the models in fashion magazines. However, we don't make judgments, as in "good" or "bad." What we do is line you up with character "types." As we walk down the street, a split-second fantasy occurs: *The woman walking her dog, what does she look like naked? Wait. I saw a woman like her in that magazine. The secretary at work looks like that.* The magazines offer tons of naughty character fantasies of secretaries and nurses, cheerleaders and lawyers, moms and doctors. (Don't tell me you don't know about this.) Unlike players, who are playing a numbers game, Bad Boys are out to enjoy a variety of types: different ethnicities, different hair colors, different body shapes, different ages, different everything. We try to enact our fantasy list the same way someone might check off items on a grocery list. Is that harsh? It's kind of true for all men. We want to find out who's naughty or nice, and enjoy both.

How can you make this work for you?

Figure out what type you fit into. There are endless options. Here are just a few:

- tomboy
- athlete
- trailer park honey
- Hooters girl
- co-ed
- secretary
- Ph.D./brainy type
- cashier
- working girl
- model

You can't always choose your type—often, it's just who you are, and it dictates which men will be attracted to you. Just look in the mirror and figure out, objectively, which type you fit best. Then you can accentuate your body language and clothes to better fit your type. The secret to your success will be figuring out what it is about that type that drives a guy nuts. Is it the way your hair's pulled back? The way your gym sweats hug your legs? Your faux glasses? Figure it out, and work it.

No, I don't expect you to go to the grocery store in a nurse's outfit, with cleavage spilling into your cart. Just be aware of our penchant for stereotypes, and if the opportunity arises, add a little something spicy to your outfit, even just around the house. Eyeglasses, tousled hair, and pigtails—however subtle, we'll pick up on it. Remember the first Britney Spears video, "Baby One More Time," where she was dressed as a schoolgirl? It makes you wonder what man was on wardrobe duty that day.

You may be saying, "Steve, this sounds similar to what you told me in the Halloween chapter, 'Halloween Tricks.'" If so, you're a smart one. I'm emphasizing certain points to show you how the things you need to know overlap, and that many of these chapters have less than six degrees of separation.

A Word on Porn and Grooming

If you want to know what men expect from women's bodies, take a peek yourself. Pornography is like a man's encyclopedia, explaining the mystery of women. Want to know how to groom "downtown"? Just look at the current trends of waxing in the magazines men read. The makers of this media are keen on knowing what large groups of men like or dislike; their sales depend on it. Since individual tastes vary, once you're with a man, you can have that talk, but in the meantime you can get a pretty good idea of bikini trends online or in the magazine section of a truck stop.

One morning my friend Ginger rang me and asked what shape she should do her bikini line in. I told her just do a "Brazilian."

She asked, "You mean shave it in the shape of Brazil, the country?"

"No," I laughed, "the style."

She was still confused, so I pulled a few pages from a "friend's" magazine, and the next time she visited, I showed her the options. Job done.

In the end, you need to do whatever you feel comfortable with, but I want you to be aware of everything men think so that you can make sober, knowledgeable decisions for yourself. It's not all pretty, but it's information you can choose to use or lose. Please don't shoot the messenger!

Chapter 19

Self-Confidence

If I love me, you will love me.

On to the next chapter.

I'm kidding. But that is a good line to repeat once a week.

Self-confidence has been, and always will be, one of the greatest challenges in life. Confidence comes and goes like the weather. It doesn't matter how rich, how famous, how hot, or how smart you are. Self-esteem is something that needs constant maintenance.

Two people who love themselves independently are much better off in a relationship than two needy people who come together out of desperation. What does this mean? *Before every relationship, you have to spend the time necessary to be happy alone before you can be happy with someone else.* Why am I telling you this? Because women who are looking for fulfillment via the validation of a man will find themselves on a roller coaster. Needy women are vulnerable, and in an incredibly weak position in a relationship. The man can essentially do whatever he wants, and the needy woman will cling, and most likely end up badly hurt. This is not how strong, wonderful, resilient relationships are created.

I've gone out with women like this, particularly women who are obviously "shopping" for a husband—which is a form of neediness. The women in such a relationship are easily manipulated. I recently dated a woman who saw all men as potential husbands, so much so that she was blind to the fact that any man who wants marriage and kids is not necessarily the right man for her. To me, she might as well have worn a sign blinking I WILL BELIEVE ANYTHING YOU SAY!

YOU CAN STRING ME ALONG! She wanted to be married so badly that she couldn't see the horrendous relationships she was walking into. I tried to tell her this, but she had a thick head. Who knows where she is now.

Men can sense if you're only half of a whole, and we, consciously or subconsciously, take advantage of this in order to further our agenda. The ball's in our court; game, set, match . . . you lose.

Consider the opposite case: We meet a woman who claims verbally or nonverbally that she is content alone. We are intrigued. We want to come after her. We want to break her down and be the one she *chooses* to be with, the one she *wants*. We are driven by the simple process of getting what we don't think is available. This scenario is where solid, wonderful, resilient relationships come from. The beauty here is that not only does this strategy help you get the guy, but it also gives you the love you deserve and the self-esteem you'll need to make a healthy relationship work.

How to Build Self-Esteem

These suggestions may sound clichéd, but enjoying life solo is the key to eventually enjoying life *en deux*.

- Do things for yourself. Buy yourself a gift. Knit a scarf, run a marathon, buy a dog. Anything.

- Entertain yourself. Cook alone, read solo in the park, go to a movie alone, or attend a concert by yourself.

- Go away for a weekend. Just you. If you're new at solo travel, try going to a spa by yourself.

- Take a class. Learn something new. Pick up a new hobby.

If you're saying, "I bought this damn book because I don't *want* to be alone," don't despair. But you may have missed the point.

With your resistance to "me time," you've become desperate. We all know what the scent of desperation smells like, and it ain't Chanel. Men can sniff it from a mile away.

All I'm asking you to do is to take a moment in your solitude and say out loud the following sentence: "I'm fun to be with. I have a good time by myself, and although it would be nice to share this time with a man, I would rather chill alone than be in a thankless relationship just to fill the hours." It's amazing the effect those words can have on your self-esteem. They're like an energy drink for your confidence organ. Didn't know you had a confidence organ? There's a lot of stuff inside you, and there's one of those, too. Find it and take care of it.

Chapter 20

From Business Card to Bombshell

You work hard for the money. There is a time and a place, however, to mix business with pleasure, and that time and place is not on a date. I'm sorry to break it to you, but we guys—and I mean all of us, both leaded and unleaded breeds—are not turned on by what you do for a living.

> Note: At best, your job title is down around number five in terms of importance . . . unless, of course, your job involves a pole and you don't work for the fire department.

It sounds callous, but our lack of interest in your work actually makes sense: Chances are, we will *never* work with you; we will instead romantically hang out with you for a few hours a day for months or for years. Therefore, your job and professional life are only marginally relevant to us, while your social skills and personality are pivotal. That being said, any man worth his salt will respect and admire a woman's place in the workforce and will want to spend time with a woman who is professionally fulfilled. But your position as a clerk or a CEO will have little bearing on your sex appeal. There are other *positions* men find more riveting.

Show Me the Honey

I have always had successful female friends who refuse to let their professional stature blend into the background when they're trying to make it work with a man. Not surprisingly, those same bossy women don't have to resist answering the dating phone—because it ain't ringing. Out there in the competitive world of work, there's little place for a sweet, sensitive lady. We all understand that. But a sweet, sensitive lady is what is needed to attract men in the world of dating. Career women often put so much time into becoming the best in their field that their career becomes their full-time identity, and everything else fades away. Guess what usually skips town first? The sexy, feminine vibe that attracts men.

That said, I love going after a hard businesswoman who won't be broken down by any man. In fact, I consider it a challenge. I proceed by hitting every feminine nerve she has, stimulating every sexual fiber in her body, saying everything that, if said in her office, would result in HR taking me away in handcuffs. But I have the time and the inclination to go after you because I like to conquer you. Another man might be too busy or too lazy to break down your walls. Give a guy a break. Don't think of it as making it easy for him; think of it as making it easy for yourself! Use your most powerful negotiating tool: the fact that you're a woman. Bombshells have more fun. If you're smart and successful, exercise the most basic truth in life: It ain't fair, you *can* have your cake and eat it, too.

What to Do

Of course, any marginally appropriate man will ask about your job. It's perfectly reasonable to answer—*briefly.*

1. Say what you do and mention your title early. Get it out of the way.

2. Weed out the weak by paying attention to his reaction and kicking him to the curb if he's rudely uninterested or conde-scending.

3. Sprinkle job talk with self-deprecating jokes and flirtation.

When you get stuck on job talk for a few minutes, choose an area that relates to what he does, and get off the topic quickly.

All About Him

When women are sizing up men, they think differently from men. They care about their man's job. Women are impressed with job titles, along with job descriptions and accompanying bankbooks—all of which can be aphrodisiacs. But just because he's blabbing on about his job and you're listening rapturously doesn't mean that you can turn the tables at the next pause in the conversation. You want to leave the briefcase mentality at the office—unless, of course, you're having a little "desk-clearing" romance. You want a man to like you for the woman, not the account executive, in you. Men are interested in one thing: *Show me the honey!*

Get Your Degree in Sexy

1. Look at being seductive as a project; go after it with the same heat with which you went after your career.
2. Pay attention to the chapters in this book on how to dress to attract a man.
3. Be selfish and spend time on your body and health.
4. Find ways to relieve stress . . . batteries may be required.

Uh-oh: Trouble on the Night Shift

There are a few scenarios in which talking about your job can help you get to the root of a man's psyche quickly, and get out while the getting out is good.

Intimidated Men

Insecure men can be intimidated by how much they assume you make, and by those three letters summarizing your position (e.g., CEO, COO, VIP). These men are to be avoided. A man's insecurity can be the tip of the "I'm a moron" iceberg looming below his "I'm not worthy" skin.

Unhappy Men

Men who are unhappy in their jobs can assume that because you're successful you are thrilled with your job and life. This makes for a hard vibe—you talk about how good your day was, and he talks about how he hates his life. If a grown man can't figure out a way to be happy, this is probably an endemic problem! You can try encouraging him, but be proud of your success, and move on.

Time to Let Your Hair Down

I have this conversation a lot:

"Steve, men are always intimidated by my job and salary."

"Every single guy you date?"

"Yeah."

Could it be, just maybe, that it's that stiff smile, the buttoned-up blouse, and that dogmatic attitude that are turning the men off? Maybe it's not him but you. I'm not suggesting that you dumb it down or behave less seriously. I am suggesting that perhaps you're too concerned with being respected and not concerned enough with being lusted after. By letting your hair down and being sexy, you are by no means relinquishing the respect you've worked so hard to achieve. Ladies, I cannot stress this enough: on your way up the corporate ladder, it's no big deal to have the guy a few rungs down look up your skirt from time to time . . . ah, now, *that's* a metaphor. We're people, not machines, and I guarantee that a healthy, sexy relationship will be just as rewarding as the title on your business card.

Chapter 21

Beauty and the Brains

I want him to love me for the inside," you say? Now's your chance. Once you have men flocking around you all hot and bothered, put on the brakes and get them to pay attention. What you have done is create options for yourself. Most of your female friends won't get this concept, so you'll have very little competition—and a fair bit of envy. You know how they say that there are two guys for every girl? Well, chances are you'll end up with four guys because some other girl didn't read this section. That's her problem. You've just doubled your chances of meeting someone who you can truly fall in love with.

As I mention at the beginning of this part, the foolproof way to get and hold on to a man is to bait him with your body and then—switch!—keep him with your brain. Now let me get specific.

The Switch

The switch happens when he goes from thinking sexsexsexsex to, "Okay, I'm not going to have sex right now. Who *is* this girl?" It will be as if he's woken up. This is where you need to engage him—and he, you. This is where you get to know each other. If you feel his attention waning, then pump up the sexy for a minute and reel him back in. If you are good at the switch, he'll never even notice it's happened. One minute he's staring at your chest, and the next he's asking about your family.

But you have to get him to pay attention to what you're saying because, even as you're speaking, he's imagining everything from how you look naked to how you kiss. The key is to let your man lust for you enough that he doesn't get bored, but not so much that he begins ignoring your voice altogether. Too much "smart talk" makes your voice sound like Charlie Brown's teacher's. In other words, if you are discussing an economic strategy for developing countries, you'd better weave in some playful comments after about fifteen minutes. Even if your date's a member of the UN, he's not going to be interested in talking about Namibia all night. You're on the date because he's interested in you physically and sexually.

Here are easy, smart conversation starters you'll both find sexy:

1. Ask him out-of-the-ordinary questions about:
- his first car
- his favorite concerts
- his favorite sports teams
- small dogs versus big dogs

2. Share opinions on various subjects, avoiding religion and politics like the plague. The best way to find out about a man is by hearing his opinion on a topic rather than by "asking him about himself." Pick a topic in the tabloids regarding a celebrity couple, talk about gas prices, or mull over the difference between people who travel and those who don't. This will engage both of you and will reveal the ways he thinks.

3. Pay attention to what he's saying by taking the focus off yourself. The first few weeks in a relationship are crucial because it's when most people inadvertently reveal themselves.

Men want sex, and a big part of sex is mental, right? (Sex is particularly mental if it's with me! But I digress.) Sex is a physical act that fulfills your mental fantasies. Chances are if you're too dry and formal in your conversation, you may turn him off by not maintaining your sex appeal. The main point here is the sex appeal, so balance the conversation between fun and function, with the fun being the flirting and the function being the info you need in order to get to know him, and vice versa.

Using Your Brains to Your Benefit

Later in the relationship, mental stimulus is the tool you can use to keep your boy in the "yard." The yard is your little playground, also known as your love life. After all, the brain is the sexiest organ of all. If you've got it, flaunt it. (I'm surprised the plastic *sturgeons*—sturgeon is a bottom-dwelling fish—haven't invented implants for that baby.)

How and when you flaunt your brains is a situational matter, but you want to remember these points:

- Smart women are funny.
- Smart women tease us.
- Brilliant women spontaneously switch gears, talk about something intelligent, and end with a naughty reference.
- Smart women know that men are prone to visual imagery and will therefore choose their words wisely so as to create the most heat without being too obvious.

By casually letting us in on the fact that you ain't dumb, you will also be keeping us on our toes. We'll second-guess ourselves before we attempt to pull some bullshit on you.

What to Do If He's Clearly Smarter than You

Even if you're dating a rocket scientist, you may know lots of things that your man doesn't: where plastic comes from, how ducks are able to fly for so long when migrating, anything. Just get him talking about a topic that he most likely won't know anything about yet will find interesting. This strategy will keep him asking himself, "What does she know that I don't know?"

I've been with women whom I thought were completely vacant, and then all of a sudden they said a few words in a foreign language, talked about ballet, did origami, or jumped into a karate pose, and it captivated me.

Men want to be *captivated.* It's part of the romantic chess game. Please don't distrust the ethics of the beauty and the brains, the bait and switch. To bait and switch is not to mislead, nor is it downplaying your own intelligence—quite the contrary. It is simply a way of exercising your knowledge of how nature works: the laws of attraction are already in place, and if you fight them you'll be stationed on Solo Island, population one. Think about it.

So let's go "fishing."

The Hunt: Boys on the Town

You probably won't like some of the information in this section, but it's the truth, and you need to know what you're facing out there so you can use it in your favor.

Imagine a tennis court. Guys—and especially Bad Boys—are like tennis players who make a shot and then run back to center court, then make another shot and run back to center court. They essentially live in center court. Why? Because the prospect of a new romantic challenge is as exciting as jumping out of a plane or driving fast. Therefore, we don't "commit" to one side of the court or the other. We want options.

Do you think I haven't been rejected? Many, many times. So many times that I've found that the best way not to feel that sting is to date at a frenetic pace. If someone steps into view who has the skills to stop me in my tracks, so be it. However, if I'm rejected, no big deal, because I'm always moving forward, and an object in motion tends to stay in motion. I'm on the road, in the passing lane, en route to finding the best way to meet and seduce the next woman.

But where do Bad Boys meet their matches? How can you snag a hot catch of your own—or two or three? This section is about the all-important first impression, and doing everything in your power to make sparks fly. Your trip to pick up your dry cleaning, groceries, or a quick meal may seem fairly routine. Men have a routine as well: we're in the routine of looking for every opportunity to approach you and fill our cell phones with yet another contact for a possible date. Some men are great at approaching women; others are not so great. But all men are opportunistic when it comes to meeting women. You can consider this part the lightbulb you need to turn on to see situations for what they really are. Just pay attention.

Keep in mind that all guys exhibit this behavior from time to time. Again, by understanding the Bad Boy, all men will become that much easier to get and keep. There will be times when the line between Bad Boy and a regular Joe is blurred, but you'll be ready for either, so don't worry.

Chapter 22

Moving in Fast

Guys approach you all the time.

"No," you say? You haven't been approached in ages?

No matter how single you think you are, I guarantee you've been approached numerous times this month, whether by a guy on a bus or a hottie in a bar. You probably weren't paying attention, weren't interested, or weren't in the mood. But the guys were there. I want to teach you exactly what men are thinking when they approach you, so that you can take the ball into your own court and control the situation. This chapter will explain how I approach women, the tricks men use in different scenarios, and how you should respond.

When I'm on the Move

When I approach a woman, I'm moving in and I'm moving in fast. There won't be hesitation or second-guessing. The best part? You'll never even see me coming. Guys skilled at the art of the approach are like great white sharks: They lurk silently, and then—wham! They're in a feeding frenzy. You won't hear lines like "Come here often?" or "Are you from the islands, because Jamaican me horny." A Bad Boy, or any decent guy, will start talking to you as if he's known you his whole life, making the interaction feel natural and meant-to-be. In retrospect, you won't even be able to recall his approach line. (*Note*: You should always feel free to use the same strategy if you want to meet a guy!)

How does a guy get so good at this "approach" thing? Men are rejected over and over again until the sting and humiliation of your cold shoulder and rolling eyes have pushed them to achieve perfection. Some guys wither and retreat, while others get smart and strong. How good are we? So good that we have ways to get *you* to come to *us*.

I'm talking about the guys who come up and just start talking, so naturally that you feel as if you're old friends. (I call this approach "pretend a friend.") They most definitely don't start with their name and a handshake. If you wait a while, you may find out whether he's just being friendly or if he likes you, but by then he will have worked every charm in the book, and by the time you realize that he does seem kind of interested, guess what? You'll be interested, too! That is our gift and our skill. And I'm going to tell you exactly how we do it, so you know what to look for while out in the jungle.

Day-to-Day Scenarios

When we see you out shopping or running errands, we study your body language in order to analyze what kind of girl you are. Let me explain: The way you dress, carry yourself, your probable age, and any other physical statistics we can pick up go into this equation. Then we categorize you. (Are you catching on yet that "types" are important to men?) We've had so much experience meeting women that we have developed very reliable categories, and we have a game plan custom-fit for you. Some samples of those categories include:

- bored girl
- overworked girl
- happy-go-lucky girl
- tomboy
- up-for-whatever girl

After we evaluate you, we move in with the idea that we'll make it up as we go along, and remain flexible in case you throw us a curveball. But we trust our instincts and experience.

We never use opening lines unless we are intentionally being corny. For example, I've walked up to a girl and disarmed her by saying in a very sarcastic voice, "Hey baby, come here often?" This instantly put the two of us on the same page. I imagined she didn't like those types of guys, and I let her know I wasn't one of them.

We try to make you feel safe as quickly as possible. We want to make you instantly comfortable around us, and we do this with the disarming tools of comedy and commiseration.

On Location: Clubs, Bars, and Beaches

These locations are by far the toughest because there women are on what I call "Wizard of Oz guard duty": No one gets to see the Wizard. No one, no how. Success in clubs, bars, or beaches depends on luck, timing, and skill . . . or alcohol.

Men have come to believe that anything we say to women, whether genuine or not, is going to be misconstrued as a lame come-on. Still, when we see you in these environments, we are driven to meet you. Here's what the pros do:

• *Pros use a female wingman to approach women easily.* Women immediately put up a wall when we approach solo, but I've always found it's ten times easier to walk up to women at bars and clubs when I'm with another woman because she creates a safety zone. I was once so bold as to ask a complete stranger to walk up with me to meet a particular woman—and she obliged. (More on this in Chapter 32.)

• *Pros approach a group of several women.* However, there's a catch here: Girls in a pack have a pack mentality. None of you wants to seem interested in front of your friends. That's when the "divide and conquer" technique comes into play. What we do is talk to the girl who seems like the low man on the totem pole, or the friendliest girl in the group. That girl serves as our "crash test dummy." If she likes us, most often her friends will warm up. Soon the group will realize that there is only one man and several of them, and they will start talking among themselves, and that's when we move on the girl we really like.

• *On the beach, pros pretend we're your brother.* We don't give off any sign of intimate interest. Why is the beach so tough? You're naked, just about! You feel vulnerable, and we can't think straight. We can't just "act casually," because we're dying inside. So, then, how do we meet you? When I'm on the beach, I run a dialogue in my head that sounds something like this: "This girl is just a friend. I couldn't care less. If she's a bitch, I'll just keep walking. It will take a minute for her to trust me, so I need to approach and be friendly but not at all flirty for the first few minutes. And, without exception, I will not let her catch me glancing at her chest, bum, or anything else." It works.

• *Pros mention an ex-girlfriend in the very beginning of the conversation.* I know. It's a no-no. You're not supposed to talk about your ex to a girl you're interested in . . . or are you? On a date, no. But we know that if we mention an ex, it will give you the sign that (a) we've had a girl, and (b) we're not sold on you. It's a show of overt confidence. This also makes us seem amateurish or not too polished—and this, my friend, takes you off guard. I remember that I once got so good at approaching women that they sensed my game. It pays to seem a little awkward.

What This Means for You

All this info is useless unless you can turn it around to work to your best interest. Here are some points to keep in mind:

• Any man who approaches you, for any reason, at any time, may well be interested in you romantically or sexually.

• Any man who approaches you has some sort of an agenda.

• Be yourself and play the player. Have fun. It's a game.

• Read men's magazines and immerse yourself in "guy" stuff as often as possible. This throws men off guard, because you'll be able to reference sports, TV, hot celebrities, or anything else "guy."

• Pretend that you are not affected by a man's approach. Meaning: you are completely comfortable, and able to look at the man with amusement, as if saying, "Okay, cute little boy, let's see what you've got for Mama." This will drive even the most skilled Bad Boy mad.

• Know that when you are in public, you are being watched. Use it to your advantage if you want to meet guys. They are looking for easy targets, so if you present yourself as a friendly, easy-to-talk-to target, they'll swoop in like flies to a Venus fly-trap.

• The approach is one of the most crucial moments in stranger-to-stranger contact. Don't fear it. Have fun with it.

• Watch men watching and approaching other women. You'll learn tons.

The object is for you to spend enough time studying male-female interaction that you become enlightened, and "what to do" becomes second nature. It's *fun*, remember?

One More Thing

Being a bitch when a man approaches you can be an effective way to weed out the weak and repel the creeps. The weak will walk away immediately, and the creeps will get what they deserve.

If you happen to have a hot body and flaunt it often, chances are you get a lot of attention from men, and use bitchiness as a way to ward off the "unsuitables." However, the more confident you are, the more likely you'll employ a buffet of tactics to separate the men from the boys. Bad Boys love a bitch because she helps us keep our edge. The tougher a woman is to crack, the more fun we have, and the better we get at seduction. To all you bitches out there (wow, that sounds like the beginning of a rap song), you'll know a Bad Boy has arrived when he hits you like a ton of bricks and leaves you laughing so hard your mascara is running . . . even the waterproof kind.

Chapter 23

What's My Line?

It's not easy being original with women these days, especially when it comes to pickup lines. Men skilled at the art of the introduction know that these first few moments are crucial. They also know that a pickup line followed by five minutes of perfect conversation will make a man's game seamless.

How do we do it? By using you. Or, I should say, using your desire to hear nice things. We understand the following points:

- All women (and men, but women more so) love compliments.

- When a woman is relishing a compliment, she's suddenly available and open-minded.

- If you have a boyfriend, he most likely stopped praising you after three months or so—which is why you're flirting with us.

- Women don't like pickup lines. It makes them feel run-of-the-mill. They prefer personalization.

- Women like to feel safe, especially with strangers.

- Women are bombarded with negative messages from the media and advertisers, messages questioning their weight, clothes, hair, makeup, faces, boyfriends, and every other aspect of their lives. We provide a welcome diversion.

Smart men know that negative advertising is part of your world. We men are "advertising" to you as well, but in a positive way. We strive to enter your planet and make you feel good. We hop off Mars, come over to Venus, and try not to act like Uranus. Simple.

How can you spot that you're being picked up by a Bad Boy? All men operate a little differently, but when I meet a woman, I like to focus on the tangible and visible features I enjoy, and compliment her on them. As we get to know each other better, I catalogue more praises so that I don't sound stale. (I love women, so this isn't difficult.) I make sure that I verbalize these things in a spontaneous fashion. Clever men will see your insecurities—scars, nose, toes, you name it—and compliment you on those, showing you that they find beauty in what you see as faults. (*Note:* Disgusting men will use your insecurities to make you feel bad about yourself. If a guy does this, dump him, pronto!)

How We Sound Original

Bad Boys are original—that's why we sound original. That doesn't mean that we haven't said similar things to other girls. We employ two main strategies, usually at the same time:

1. We personalize our message to make you believe that we're telling the truth. We are keenly aware that a woman's instinct is strong, and if she senses bullshit, she will put the wall back up. So we use information you've already told us about yourself, such as cracking jokes about the company you work for or swearing that we love your favorite beer.

2. We talk to you straight. We know that you've heard all the crap before, and realize that the best way to your heart and your bed is by being refreshingly candid. We talk to you as a friend, without ever being so friendly that the relationship loses its sex appeal.

Why Men Work So Hard at Pickup Lines

Men control what they say and how they say it for one reason: power in the relationship. Their primary goal is to get from A to B. A smart man knows that a woman floating on a compliment cloud is more malleable and therefore more likely to see things "his way." A woman's desire to feel good about herself is equivalent to a man's desire to have sex; it's that strong, and we know it. Both men and women want to be in control, and having the right lines is an important step in that direction. The good news is that complimenting works both ways.

What This Means for You

Take the damn compliment! Feel good. You deserve it. Plus, chances are he actually means it! Then get your feet back on the ground and pay attention. Men like compliments, too. (Later in the book, in Chapter 25, I'll tell you how you can say the right lines at the right time.)

In general, remember that when a man compliments you, it's his way of multitasking; he is making you feel good *and* trying to get the upper hand. The only other time you'll find a man multitasking is when he's kissing you and, at the same time, undoing your bra.

Chapter 24

Open for Business 24/7

My female friends often list excuses as to why they *didn't* approach an attractive guy in a bar: he was married, he seemed to be tired after work, he had just dined with another woman, etc. Let me tell you something important: *all* men are approachable—even men in committed relationships. If he is decent, a man will talk to you politely no matter what, and the committed ones will leave your advances without the exchange of digits or e-mail addresses. The reason for this is simple: any man approached by a woman is flattered by her overture. The social rule is that men come up to women, and when you switch that around, it's a home run for us guys.

The only men you should not approach are men in tuxedos walking alone down a church aisle, men in handcuffs being led away by police, men walking hand in hand with other men, men with their wife and/or children, and celebrity men. Everyone else is fair game.

And anytime/anyplace is fair game. Weddings, funerals, bus stops, self-serve gas stations, Laundromats, churches, temples, hospital waiting rooms, and the line at the DMV—these are all places where men are willing to engage the opposite sex. Guys are always on the "lookout." Like convenience stores, some men are classy and

> Note: Think of men as convenience stores: *We are open 24 hours a day, 365 days a year.*

well serviced; others are scummy and to be avoided. You can tell the difference just by looking in the window. There are three great ways to get your Slurpee . . . er, to approach us:

1. Aggressive, then back away
2. Oh, I need help
3. Safety in numbers

1. Aggressive, Then Back Away

One of the sexiest things a woman ever did was come up to me, grab me by the front of my shirt like she was going to beat me up, and say, "You're a biscuit." Which in Capetown, South Africa, means you're attractive. Then she walked away, giggling. Of course I went and found her. She remains a close friend to this day. Her approach worked because her confidence was sexy, she'd caught me off guard, and she was a refreshing change. Any exciting, confident version of this will work in your favor. For example, you could walk up to a guy and say, "You, me, we need to talk." Keep in mind that timing and location are key—don't grab a cop or your boss. Walk up to a guy and hand him your phone number and say, "I'm [your name] and this is my number. Call me." Then smile and walk away. Women don't normally do this, so it will completely take him by surprise. If he likes you, he'll call, but either way, you just stood way above the average woman. The point isn't whether he calls, but that you're being proactive.

2. Oh, I Need Help!

"Oh, I need help!" is an ancient ploy, first documented in silent movies as the damsel-in-distress role. Nowadays, women don't need men like they used to; you're all independent. Therefore, if you come up to us and genuinely have a question, be it about driving directions, a do-it-yourself project, or a "why guys do such-and-such," we are more than happy to oblige. We want to help. It works because it feeds our egos. We haven't had to go to the trouble of approaching you, and yet we still feel important. Ask away!

3. Safety in Numbers

"Safety in numbers" is when a group of women approach one or two men. This intimidation tactic is priceless. You're hitting *us* with your mass presence. You not only have the ball in your court, but you have the court itself. The best part is that you don't have to wait for the guys to leave if you don't like them; *you* do the splitting. You can move around a party, a mall, or a bar and have fun all night, all without the social pressure of trying to carry on awkward conversations alone.

Warning: Come prepared with an exit strategy that will leave the losers with their egos intact. A few choice words such as "You guys were great, but it's ladies' night, so we'll see you later" should do the trick. It won't hurt to make a pact between the ladies involved in case one of you likes a guy. The best strategy is to all leave together for a preplanned "engagement" and have your friend make plans with the cutie for a later date. But leave as a group!

Approaching a man, though unconventional, is highly effective. Keep in mind that with all of these strategies, the basic tenor of your interaction should be you making the approach, then sitting back and letting us do the work. We still want to be able to hunt you. *So once you've made that initial introduction, let us hunt.* Also, even if you are rejected, you will learn an immense amount about a man's world. We are constantly shut down in our pursuit of happiness with women, so do not take rejection personally. Just think of it as another step toward understanding a man's world, and use it to your advantage. I use this analogy: People are like ice cream. Just because someone doesn't like your flavor doesn't mean you're not tasty to someone else!

Q&A

Q: If a guy isn't married by the time he's forty, is there some-thing wrong with him?

A: Yeah, he's smarter than other forty-year-old men! No, there's nothing wrong with him. He may not want kids, and for many women that's a deal breaker. However, if he still lives with his mom or has never had a multiyear relationship, you may have a point. Still, in many ways, you may be at an advantage, because he most likely has a lot of dating experi-ence, and knows how to handle his own home and affairs.

Q: What about going out with younger guys or men who are from a different culture than my own?

A: That's a two-part question. To answer the first part: the younger the guy, the more immature he'll most likely be. However, if you take that into consideration and go into it thinking he may be fun for a while, then it's fine. In general, women mature faster than men, and the age difference could pose certain problems. But, by all means, give it a shot, because he may turn out to be mature beyond his years. Coo coo kichoo, Mrs. Robinson.

The second part of your question is answered simply. If you are attracted to him, go out with him. Bad Boys are "equal opportunity" employers; we like to date across age and ethnic barriers to gain full knowledge of *all* women, and from there we make our decision as to who fits the best with our particular set of interests and standards. That attitude would be something I recommend you adopt.

Chapter 25

Practice Flirting

Flirting is to relationships like water is to showering. Really, it's that important. Pivotal. It's not the soap or the razor or the adorable pink loofah. It's the water. Learning to be an effective, gracious flirter will solve 85.93 percent of your dating woes. (This is a statistically accurate figure.) That's because people who flirt well tend to be in the driver's seat, and people in the driver's seat get to drive, and people who drive can steer the relationship. I'll explain.

If you were to follow a successful person through her entire life, you would see that the art of flirting—and it is an art—is often applied in every arena of her existence. It's how she forges business relationships, how she meets and brings out the "fun" in new friends, and how she lets people see her sexy side. Effective flirters are successful people, romantically, professionally, and socially.

> **Flirt** (v.) To behave in a playfully alluring way. (n.) 1. somebody who behaves in a playfully alluring way. 2. you, from now on.

In this chapter, I'm going to teach you step by step how to flirt with every man, woman, and beast in your path until you are a flirting guru.

The Mentality Behind Flirting

Flirting doesn't always have to have sexual or romantic overtones. Its primary purpose is to solicit playfulness. So, in your head, you need to think *fun*. You are going out to have fun with people until they laugh and become engaged. Not all of us are comedians, but every one of us knows how to compliment someone and ask questions to show we're interested. It's that simple. Think *fun* and *light*. That's your agenda.

For example, once I was in a crowded restaurant waiting for a table—something I don't like to do. The hostess was visibly flustered, and considered the waiting patrons to be an angry mob. I approached her and recommended a trapdoor at the dining tables so that when someone was finished eating, they would drop through the floor and not sit there all night making it difficult for her to seat new guests. She laughed, put my group at the next available table, and Miss Grumpy Hostess and I dated for a few months. Success! Happiness is flirting, and flirting is happiness.

When to Flirt

Be ready to flirt anytime, anywhere. Okay, so don't do it at funerals or at work, where it can get you into big-time sexual harassment trouble. Everywhere else is fair game. I flirt with everyone: cashiers, waitresses, delivery people, neighbors, cops, toll booth operators, telemarketers, you name it. It's all about having fun with a stranger, whether male or female, and seeing them break into a smile.

I know what you're thinking: Why would I flirt with someone of the same gender? Well, I'm straight—obviously—but I will often joke around with gay men, and will feel completely masculine doing so, because I know it's all just fun. You're just having a good time and making good connections. My point is that you have opportunities every single waking hour to flirt, and very few people should be left out of the mix. Plus, you'll find that flirting makes you feel as good as it does the other person.

Secret: If you're not in the mood to be social, don't go out to flirt. Flirting takes a carefree attitude, and if you're not feeling particularly happy, then it's best to lay low. Even I'm not in the mood for it sometimes.

What Am I Doing Again?

You'll know you have flirted successfully when the person standing across from you *feels good about himself.* Always keep that in mind. Flirting is about the other person. While self-deprecating humor is okay, you're focusing on *the other person,* not yourself.

Q&A

Q: How do I stop him from flirting with my friends?

A: You break his legs. I'm kidding. Flirting is healthy. However, if he's taking it too far, let him know privately that it bothers you. If he doesn't change, dump him.

But I've Never Been Good at Flirting

If you're a flirt-a-phobe, practice on people who are paid to talk to you: store employees. My practice arenas are those enormous department stores such as Wal-Mart. Minimum-wagers are often bored and ready to babble. Other great locales are grocery stores, gas stations, hardware stores, and any store in a mall.

1. Pick someone who is stocking a shelf or doesn't look too busy (that shouldn't be too difficult).

2. Walk up and start talking to him or her about anything. Pick something to do with the weather, the store you're in, or gossip about something you saw or heard on the news (but avoid politics). For example, try "Excuse me, do you think it would be odd to use mouse traps as bag clips?"

3. Find a way to compliment him or her. This may not be easy if you're talking to the human disaster stocking the hemorrhoid cream shelves, but most people have at least one redeeming quality. Find it and compliment it. For example: "You only have one tooth, but at least it's clean" or "It's great you were able to get this job after being in prison for so long." Or, on a serious note, "You seem really smart and charming. There's no way this job can keep you. You'll be off running your own company soon."

4. Try to get him or her to smile or laugh. The best way to do this is to find out what TV shows or movies he or she watches. Rehash a scene from a movie and discuss why it was so funny. This works for several reasons, but the most salient reason it works on guys is that we men often feel that women don't share our same "sick" sense of humor. When you start quoting from our favorite shows, we feel "understood."

5. Keep your contact short and sweet and move on to the next victim.

6. After flirting your way through several employees, try to strike up a conversation with a stranger/fellow customer.

Not everyone will respond to you—I'm attractive and personable, and people ignore me all the time—so in the beginning, take your ego out of it. Don't feel hurt if not everyone wants to talk to you. Just keep it moving.

You're Not Good at It, But You Flirt Anyway

Most poor flirters lack the ability to *read* people. As a result, they either insult their target, step over boundaries, or overstay their welcome. If you're getting more rejection than acceptance in the flirting department, then remember these things:

- Be sure that you're looking well groomed and attractive.
- Don't get too personal.

- Make your interaction short and sweet; always leave them wanting more.
- Keep it friendly and a little less sexual.
- Pick different types of people to flirt with.

Tricks from the Pros

The pros are good at flirting for one reason: they *practice*. Women often tell me that they never have anything to say when flirting with a new guy—that's because they haven't practiced enough!

A flirting pro:

1. constantly keeps his/her engine warm by flirting with people from ages eight to eighty;

2. picks tough people to flirt with in order to raise his game (e.g., anyone who works in a customer service position most likely hates people; if you can get *them* to smile, you're a guru); and

3. separates flirting techniques into categories depending on the desired outcome:

- practice flirting;
- getting-something-for-free (or cheaper) flirting;
- meeting-someone-and-getting-a-phone-number flirting (my favorite);
- building-a-business-contact (or friend) flirting; and
- being-remembered-as-outrageous-or-funny flirting.

The Biggest Reason to Flirt

When you become accustomed to interacting with everyone, you suddenly see the entire world as approachable. Others will begin to talk to you because you are easy to talk to. Opportunities and situations will suddenly appear, all thanks to flirting. (This is actually very true—extroverts statistically have many more career opportunities than introverts.)

Flirting in a Relationship

Although your flirtatious attitude may need tempering once you're in a relationship, flirting is something that also serves as playful interaction between you and your partner, whether while cooking or on vacation. It brings fun and enjoyment to the relationship and, in virtually every scenario, is a skill that can't be replaced. Each person has a unique personality and corresponding flirting strategy, but everyone has the capacity to flirt, and should do so at the drop of a hat. The world is a better place with lots of flirting.

Chapter 26

Checkout

I have a secret to share with you: the grocery store is on my top-five list of places to meet women. Why? Because grocery shopping is a necessity. All the women in the neighborhood *must* go to the grocery store. I know that sooner or later, the attractive women on my block will be roaming the aisles.

I also know that most women don't have their guard up while shopping, nor do they expect me to be watching them. But the reason the grocery store is special is because it's one of those rare wholesome public places where people feel relatively safe. Even better? I can easily see your "current status" by what you have in your basket or cart.

How You Should Think at the Grocery Store

The word *necessity* should forever be at the forefront of your psyche when it comes to groceries. As soon as you hear the clanging of metal carriages and squeaking wheels, you should immediately think:

- It's a necessity that I look casually sexy, even if I'm just going in to pick up a few items.

- It's a necessity that I be aware that I and what's in my basket are being watched.

• It's a necessity that I don't waste this opportunity to stroll up and down the aisles to see what's on sale. And by "what's on sale," I mean "if there are any hot guys shopping."

• It's a necessity that I strike up a conversation with men who are also shopping alone. Make a fun comment on something in his basket, or try "Excuse me, do you know what aisle the coffee's in?"

• It's a necessity that I look at the grocery store as a dating arena, and not just a place to get "bread" . . . oops, pardon the breeding pun.

How We Read Your Cart

If these items are in your basket, you might as well have a neon sign above your head flashing I'M SINGLE!:

• Single servings of chicken or frozen dinners. (My friend Arianne disagrees—she is not single and yet buys frozen dinners. But I would assume that she's single "enough.")

• Small amounts of produce, such as one or two tomatoes.

• Too much cat or dog food. This is scary, because it means you have too many pets.

• No junk food whatsoever. Or a basketful of diet products. Men eat junk food. If you had one in the house, you would buy him some.

• A lonely pint of ice cream.

You're most likely dating if:

• A sixpack of non-light beer sits on top of the cheese and crackers in your cart.

• Ingredients for a meal are purchased all at once. (This also tells me you don't cook often . . . frown.)

• The movie you've just picked up is in with your groceries.

• You have the rushed and intense look of a woman getting ready for a date.

• There is a man shopping with you lovingly rubbing your back.

You don't want to be bothered if:

• Diapers fill the bottom of the carriage, and a baby is screaming topside. (Note how observant I am.)

My point is that men watch women in the grocery store as much as, if not more than, in other places. It's the easiest way for us to get the 411 on your lifestyle without your ever opening your mouth. We will even shop at various times of the day, over weeks on end, to see when the highest concentration of hotties is in a shop. Ever see a guy buying just one thing? He's not at the grocery store for the gum.

How to Check Off *Your* Grocery List

Why, if you're a single woman, wouldn't you use the exact same grocery-store tactics as Bad Boys? You should! Okay, so the lighting's not the best, but you may just find a man there.

Here's your checklist:

1. Try shopping at various times and on different days, making mental notes on when you see the most guys.

2. Look great—and friendly.

3. Shop with a girlfriend (who already has a boyfriend). Two women having fun shopping together is very attractive to a man.

4. Stay off your phone.

5. Visit the right aisles. Men like the beer aisle; less so the diaper aisle. Avoid meeting a guy near feminine hygiene products or anything phallic (bananas, cucumbers, and a long French baguette would fall under this category). It makes it hard for men to concentrate . . . the guy may want to crack up.

6. Walk slower than normal.

7. Strike up conversations.

There is no set way to meet and get asked out by someone. I'm going to repeat this over and over again. There are no hard-and-fast rules on how to act or how to "be." Being relationship-worthy is a way of life, a mentality. As I say in the introduction, it's something to study and soak in, and then store in the back of your mind. And it just so happens that the grocery store is a wonderful classroom.

Chapter 27

An Exercise Bike Built for Two

Good news: The gym is no longer a place you force yourself to go after work. Instead, it's a great place to get all hot and bothered! Your heart rate is up, everyone is showing a little skin, and you're surrounded by pumped-up men. Face it: This creates an environment where people are looking at one another in a sexual way. And that environment happens to be a great place to locate your next catch.

Think about it: Even though you're working on your inner health, you're also developing a muscle-toned exterior. Hundreds of people around you share the same motivation. Therefore, it's only reasonable to assume that some of you may be attracted to *one another*. Case in point: I've met some amazing women in the gym!

The gym is a great place to scout out potential mates, but you can't always expect them to approach you, even if they like what they see. Instead, you need to take advantage of the fact that you're in an arena where it's easy for women to break some social codes and take charge of the introduction. If you want to talk to a man in the gym, it's as simple as walking up and saying hi. Years ago, men used to approach women here, just like everywhere else. But as the popularity of gym life grew, so did the clichés of men "working" women more than working out. The result? Women got sick of it, men got far more eye rolls than phone numbers, and now we're all a little gun-shy.

As of late, attitudes are calming down a bit, and people are more receptive to meet-and-greets alongside the weights. But the gym is a woman's world now. A man might pull up beside you, but he's probably not going to say anything, so it's better if you initiate the talking. If he doesn't come near you, don't think he doesn't have the courage or interest. He might be like me, and not want you to think he's aggressively hitting on you. (Just because I say hi doesn't mean I'm trying to get in your spandex. I might just be saying hi, trying to start an easy conversation.) Men often feel that if they approach a woman, she'll immediately go into a defensive mode. It's far too complicated to explain that we are just saying hi because we're interested, so we don't bother approaching you at all.

Gym Pros and Cons

Pros
- You are being watched by lots of men. If you're single, this is a good thing.

- You are among like-minded, health-conscious people.

- You can see what he looks like all "pumped up."

- The gym is well lit, and there is no alcohol involved. This is a major plus for women who aren't into the bar scene.

- If you don't have the courage to say hello upon first sighting, you can be pretty sure you'll see him again. You can also use frequent sightings to your advantage by making eye contact one day, smiling another day, and then finally stopping to introduce yourself. It also means you'll figure out his schedule and dress accordingly . . .

- Men are easy to meet because we spend more time with weights—and stand around in between sets. If you're shy, just pretend you want to use our machine between one of our sets. Or, better yet, ask how the machine works, which will encourage two things: (a) a longer conversation and (b) the guy's feeling useful and masculine.

Cons

- He's going to check you out from head to toe.

- If you end up dating and things go badly, you'll still have to see him regularly at the gym.

- You'll have to get over the fact that men don't really care if you're sweating or not. That's your issue. Sweat is part of a man's world, and we're not bothered by it. (Sometimes it's kinda hot.)

- The gym is well lit, and there's no alcohol involved . . .

- People are often on the move from one exercise to another. Therefore, picking the right timing for an introduction can be tricky.

Get Off the Treadmill

While men often lift weights and rest between sets, women spend more time on cardio machines. Let me tell you, it's not easy to talk to a woman on a treadmill, or to a woman in a yoga class. Wanna meet more men? Start working out near the equipment that men use, such as Nautilus and free weights. At the very least, pick the cardio machine at the end of a row, along the aisle. Or join a co-ed boxing or muscle-building class. We'll start talkin' to ya, I promise.

Talky Talk

The gym is one of the few places where it's socially acceptable to strike up a brief conversation with *anyone*. If a guy sees you joking with the woman working out next to you, he'll be more likely to approach you. You know the talkative woman in your aerobics class who talks to everyone, men and women alike? She probably began by talking to women, and the men joined in the conversation. Try it.

Post Workout

Most gyms have a place where you can buy a drink or hang out after your workout. This creates an ideal place to strike up a conversation. Simply approach your man and say, "Hi, my name is [name here]. I didn't want to bother you during your workout . . ."

The beauty of the gym is that it's a win-win situation for you. You are going to work out *anyway,* for *you,* and if you meet someone during one of your visits, all the better. But if not, no big deal because that's not really why you joined. The gym is just a great place to kill two birds with one stone, should the opportunity knock.

Chapter 28

You Can Do It, and I Can Help

This book is about being proactive in every aspect of the relationship world, and in no place is this more easily achieved than in the thirty-thousand-square-foot male holding pens known as "construction supply centers." I'm talking about stores such as Home Depot and Lowe's. These places make it so easy for women to meet men that they should be considered training wheels for women who were previously too shy to approach a guy. Almost any woman can engage a guy in conversation here.

Why Construction Stores?

When I want to meet women, I go to the places with the highest concentration of women, such as lingerie shops and shoe stores. Sadly, it's a little too obvious for me to spend time in a women's shoe store cruising chicks. But you're in luck. When you want to meet men, you should go to where they are in the biggest supply, and construction supply stores have the highest concentration of men, period. And women sailing among the endless aisles of painting supplies and prefab molding can always legitimately be there for weather *stripping* and some *caulk*. You can operate incognito all you want!

Not only that, but many men will go to these places just to browse or to pick up only one or two items, which means that they're in their natural habitat, and they have time to talk. This is your chance to move in. I'm going to tell you how to do this, but you have to promise me that you'll wrap your mind around the overall philosophy behind the opportunity—*you* are becoming *proactive* and taking dating *into your own hands*—and not just memorize a set of instructions or rules. I want the things I teach you to become part of your psyche, as the new you interacts with men on her own terms.

Where to Loiter

• Men know that most women in Lowe's or Home Depot will head straight for the **painting or gardening sections.** Often, if I'm looking for damsels in "repair distress," I'll go there first to strike up a conversation. But don't forget that I'm a Bad Boy who is going to pounce as often as possible, in any section of a hardware store. Most of the guys I know can be seen cruising the plant and paint supply sections. However, there are better places in the store if you're a woman looking to meet a man.

• I rarely see women in the **lumber section,** where there are dozens of men just milling around. Clean-cut, rugged carpenter types abound—these are the guys a lot of women love.

• The **plumbing section** is great because everybody has plumbing problems. If a woman is strolling this section alone, chances are she needs a hand. Whether or not this is the case, go with it. Nothing is sexier than being surrounded by men and pipes.

• What's known as the **fastener section** is perfect because this is where there's the highest traffic flow of men. A fastener is anything that attaches two things together—think screws, nuts, hinges, nails. Everyone needs them, and therefore the aisle where they're located is usually the most crowded in the store. Feel free to have a shotgun approach in this aisle, and talk to as many men as you want. Ask lots of questions. ("I am trying to hang a really heavy painting. What do I need?" "I need to attach a cabinet to a wall. Help.")

• The **power tool** aisle is where you'll find the most men day-dreaming. If you like the handyman type, then hang out here.

Finding a Good Match

Do you have home-related interests, such as gardening or kitchen design? Stick to the section of the store that best represents those interests. Think about it—it's so much better than online dating, because the store is helpfully broken up into sections. Once you're in your area of interest, you may just find the men who have those interests, too.

To-Do List

1. Look around your home and come up with a fun little project. Why not improve your life while you're trying to meet men? Surely the bathroom could use a new coat of paint.

2. Head to the biggest hardware store you can find.

3. Warm up your engine by talking to the store help and getting advice on your project.

4. Spot a customer you want to talk to and cut right in without a formal introduction. At the most, say, "Excuse me." Then ask a question about your project, such as "Do you know if I can paint over a latex-painted wall with an oil-based paint?"

5. If there's interest from the man you've picked, you'll know right away, because he'll take over the conversation and begin pursuing questions unrelated to your initial inquiry. For example, he may respond with "You can paint over latex with oil but it's not a good idea. Better to stay with latex. Doesn't your boyfriend know about this?"—to test your "availability." If not, keep moving.

6. Keep the conversation fun and light. If you like him, tell him to get in touch with you to find out how the project turned out (i.e., give him your e-mail address or phone number). It's good to have a business card already planted in your pocket for this purpose . . . but not already in your hand. At least "pretend" to search for the card. Hand him the number and say, "You can come over for a shower when I'm done," and laugh. This says, loud and clear, that you're flirting. He'll tell everyone about the encounter. You've just made his day.

7. Be creative. If you really like the guy, tell him you would pay him to help you with your project. Offering money makes him see that you're not trying to get too much free advice. You might say, "Thanks, you've made me feel more confident. Do you know how to paint? I would pay you if you would be interested in helping me." Even if he's not interested in the job, he'll see you as a woman who isn't a user, and that's a good thing.

Another Way to Approach

1. Be very informal and assertive. If you're in the tool section, try "What's the difference between a twelve-volt and sixteen-volt drill for regular home use?" If you're in the lumber section, you might kick it off with "Why the hell is plywood so expensive?" The reason you talk like this is because it's the way guys talk to one another. It's a comfortable, conversational tone for us.

2. Listen to his response and have another question ready.

3. If you like him, say thanks and ask him his name.

Note: As I hinted at earlier, one thing men are wary of in these stores is a woman trying to get free advice or free hardware work. Do not come off as a moocher. Do not give the impression that you are just working him for construction tips, and are then going to dump him after you get what you want. Again, if you are genuine, and have a real do-it-yourself project in mind, he'll want to help. But no one wants to feel like he has SUCKER written across his forehead.

Best Times to Go

- mid- to late-afternoon on weekends;
- late Friday and Saturday nights;
- after work on weekdays; and
- very early in the morning Monday through Friday, to catch real construction tradesmen.

Hammer that store until you nail down a great guy. (Yes, I'm paid by my publisher for the number of puns I can come up with per chapter.)

Chapter 29

Take the Plunge (and the Wave and the Jump)

L ook at the size of that wave!"

"Look at that girl. Hell, she's hot."

These two statements sum up the dilemma for guys who enjoy adventure sports: we spend a lot of time in locales where few women tread. That sucks. To make matters worse, the right girl can give us the same heart-pounding exhilaration that we find in our chosen sport. We're often swayed by the fact that our sport tends to cause us less stress than women, so most of us, if we had to make a choice, would choose the wave over the babe. Sorry, girls, but waves, dirt, skate parks, and snow don't give us a hard time when we are gone for hours and having fun with our friends. Still, the fact remains that *girls* create a very similar blood flow.

So, now what? We want women and solid adventure. We have the choice to date the few girls who hang around our beach or to import a woman into our passion by teaching her how to kite, surf, ride a motorcycle, or skate. If we choose to go out with one of the few girls who frequent the surf beach, we know the odds are in her favor that she'll meet someone else due to the heavy demand. Hence the expression "You don't lose your girlfriend, you lose your turn." We prefer to date without the "turns."

Getting Action

I mentioned this earlier, but it's worth repeating: active guys love tomboys who look as great in jeans, a T-shirt, and a ponytail as they do in a dress. Australian women and surfer girls have this look down to a science, but do they have the sexy mannerisms and behavior to match? A girl can put on anything she wants, but she's still going to have to act like a girl from time to time. Here are tips for the ladies:

• Keep your style simple and sexy, but not slutty. T-shirt and jeans? Great. A T-shirt that has a picture of a kitten and says NICE PUSSY? Slutty.

• Pay attention to the way guys think, and try to wrap your mind around why we think the way we do. This will defuse potential miscommunication. Watch his eyes when he's putting his gear together for an outing or the way he talks about his sport. This will give you a visceral indication of how passionate he is about it and help you see that he's different from other men in that he thrives on living on the edge.

• If you're dating an adventurous guy, be tough with him. These guys are strong and don't like any weakness, even from their girlfriends. That means setting respectful ground rules right away and enforcing them. (But no nagging!)

• It's okay to be a "guy's girl," but not one of the guys. We don't want to date a dude, so keep the farting and spitting for your girls' night out.

• The grass isn't always greener: Don't date every guy on the beach. Your reputation as a ho will grow faster than the hair on a koala's ass!

Chapter 30

Night Moves

By now, you know how guys act at night: they get a few drinks in them, the big head becomes clueless, and the little head does all the thinking. And there's no better place to see these little Einsteins in action than at a bar.

Horrible come-on lines abound: "Don't I know you?" "Do you want a Jell-O shot?" Yadda yadda. Nevertheless, the fact remains that many of you go out to bars and clubs, and boys are part of the action. This chapter is all about knowing what to look for and how to separate the boys from the men. The idea here is that you have the last laugh. After all, there may be a decent guy in the place, but he may be a needle in a haystack.

I don't want to get your hopes up: in all my years of going out, I've probably met only a half-dozen women I would consider wonderful girlfriends at nighttime hotspots. Your chances of meeting quality people are much higher at parties hosted by friends or during daytime activities, such as professional lunches, gym workouts, and grocery shopping. It's rare to meet someone in a bar.

That said, here's how to tell the difference between the good, the useless, and the ugly at a watering hole.

The Ugly

The ugly guy is the one usually found in a pack of drunk guys who are pushing one another around, looking over at you, and laughing before one of them approaches you. The reason they act like this is that they hate rejection, particularly public rejection. So they psyche themselves up on alcohol and testosterone before they make a move so as to cushion the blow. If one of these guys approaches you, the best way to handle it is not to be a bitch; that just fuels the fire. Be polite and just tell him that you are either with someone or you are in the middle of a conversation and maybe you'll talk to him later.

The Useless

The useless guy is the one who may be seen on his own or hanging with just one other male friend. He carries himself with a strange stalker-like quality. Don't worry, you'll definitely pick up on it. You're a woman; trust your instincts. The best thing to do if this guy approaches you is to tell him that you're just having a girls' night out. If that doesn't work, mention that your boyfriend is a psycho and you never know if he'll show up. Then turn a shoulder to him.

The Good

This is *the* guy. The needle in the haystack. He was sick of sitting in his house and decided to come out. He will most likely be with a group of women or with one other woman. Pay attention, and something will tell you that the woman he's with isn't his girlfriend.

We all know that a female friend makes meeting women much easier for a man. I used this type of camouflage for years. But it's obvious when a good guy really likes you: he'll talk to you over the music for long enough to get an idea of who you are, and then tell you that he would like to see you again. If you like him, arrange a daytime meeting, such as lunch or coffee. You'll get to see him completely sober in the light of day. If he agrees to this, you may have met a good guy. If he doesn't want to see you for lunch or coffee, then he had better have a damn good excuse. If you must, meet him for dinner or a drink with a strict curfew. The date should last only ninety minutes to two hours. (More on dating in Part IV.)

How Bad Boys Operate at Bars

Bad Boys will often hang out in the background and watch how other men approach you. This tells us a few things, including what approaches are successful, how you respond (polite? bitchy? friendly?), and how easy you are. Look around and see who's watching you, and then you'll know who the interested Bad Boys are in the house.

How to Meet Men at Bars

This takes a bit of planning, but try sending out an e-mail to your friends that says, "Hey, I'm thinking of hitting X bar tomorrow night. You should come down after work and bring your friends." This is one way to make the bar scene work for you: friends date friends of friends successfully.

Warning

Safety Steve here! Before you go out with your girlfriends, always have a plan that includes:

1. a designated driver;
2. an exit strategy—don't leave any of your female soldiers behind; and
3. a down-one plan—if one of your girlfriends wants to hook up, get an exact name, address, and phone number of the guy she's leaving with, and call her up upon your arrival home.

And, finally, do not get plastered. I know I've said this before, but it deserves repeating. It's dangerous, stupid, and unattractive. Tipsy is okay, but drunk is dumb. The only reason we want to see you drunk is because we know it will be easy to have sex with you.

You'll have a lot more fun, and feel much better, if you mix in a glass of water here and there. And you may even remember your fun the next day.

Don't forget to make sure you watch your drink being poured, and never leave a drink unattended, even if you go to the bathroom. Sadly, drugged drinks are common.

This may sound a bit excessive to some of you, but it takes a split second for a fun evening to turn into a disaster. Making these plans takes only a minute or two, and they're worth it!

Chapter 31

Love Online?

Until recently, I considered online dating to be something that other people did. However, leaving no stone unturned in my research for this book, I decided to join an online dating service. I'll admit that in my month online, I met some amazing women. I also met some extremely "unique characters." My first observation? Cyberspace is filled with a lot of black holes—particularly between the ears of the people filling out profiles.

In general, the online dating world is primarily populated by people seeking sex. I could safely estimate that sex is the motivation for about 60 percent of women online, and 85 percent of men. That's not to say that there aren't great people looking for deeper relationships. But you have to use your profile, your pictures, and those oh-so-important first e-mails to advertise what you are looking for. Remember, online dating services couldn't care less whether you hook up or not—all they want is your money. What I'm getting at is that you're on your own. Well, you *were* on your own. Now *I'm* with you. I'm going to give you a little help. Let's get you into online dating shape with some simple steps.

Pictures Need to Show Your Curve Appeal

Your photo is *the* most important part of your profile and will determine what sorts of admirers you attract. Most people make the mistake of veering in one of two directions: (1) horrible, unflattering photos—often with pets, or (2) pictures featuring outfits and poses reminiscent of porn stars.

Now, I'm a dog guy, but I can tell you that I don't appreciate a woman who poses with her pet. It makes me question her sanity and consider her potentially desperate. Nor am I attracted to women who present all their "assets" in a photo, a sure sign of a woman who doesn't think she has any other assets to offer. These photos are guaranteed to attract the wrong sorts of men. Both advertising strategies erase any chance of your meeting the kind of guy you want.

Instead, you want to put up a handful of flattering photos— that's right, *multiple* photos—with one showing a little cleavage and sexiness. Of course, sexy photos are a double-edged sword. A *bit* of skin will get you noticed, but you need to balance such shots with tamer pretty photos. Your sexy photos cannot be your entire ad.

What, you're not a model? You don't photograph well? You hate having your picture taken? Excuses! Read on.

Picture Perfect

You may notice that celebrities often appear in photographs posing with three basic looks: smiling, sexy, and serious. Though they're famous, they're not models. They've had teams of industry professionals give them the 411 on their best looks and angles. You can do the same thing without the expense of a fashion crew. You will, however, need to borrow or buy a digital camera to get some perfect pics.

I've been a model for twenty years and know a thing or two about getting a good photograph. Here's the easy way to get your- self lookin' good online:

1. Take a couple of hours alone or with a male friend, and try on everything in your wardrobe to see what you look best in. (Did you notice that I said "male friend"? You're trying to attract men, so you need an honest male opinion.)

2. With one of these outfits on, take a half hour to try different hairdos and makeup schemes in the mirror. Remember that you can wear heavier makeup on film than your normal amount, if you feel it's necessary.

3. Once you have at least five outfits that you believe show off your best assets, set aside a special day for having your picture taken. It's best that the photographer be someone you feel extremely comfortable with. Do not go out and hire a professional. Pick a creative friend who knows how to take a picture.

4. Snap away! Models take literally hundreds of shots to get just one good photo. Hundreds! So keep taking pictures of yourself until you start to see a pattern of good shots. One of the secrets of modeling is "working the light," so pay attention to where your light source is, and make sure it's flattering your face and body. Aim to get at least ten great pictures, and narrow them down from there.

5. Make sure the pictures you choose reflect your sexiness and spirit. You should be seen looking as hot as possible, laughing and having fun.

Pro-File

The best way to find out about someone is not from their hobbies and interests. Instead, you'd like to know their opinions on things. With this in mind, your profile should reflect your opinions on the things that matter to you. I would avoid religion, politics, and sex. Just write about a recent activity that was important to you, or a new movie that got you thinking. Here are some other ideas:

- Pick a current issue, television show, or location, and express an opinion on it.

- Describe what you did last summer.

- Talk about what you cooked this week and why you liked it.

- Write about how it feels to get into a nice warm bed.

- Ask a question in your profile, and give your answer to that same question. My favorite: What would you rather be able to do, fly or be invisible? Why?

People looking for love want to see that you share some values and interests with them. Give hints in your profile. Remember that anyone looking for love online has found that traditional methods or time constraints have left him empty-handed. Help yourself, and the men reading your profile, by standing out from the crowd. It may be cyberspace, but it's a lot like a crowded bar.

Check Out the Competition

One of the more fun things to do is scope out the competition. Type in your own demographic information and search for a woman. This way, you will see exactly what a guy sees when searching for your "type." If you see a woman's picture or profile that really grabs your attention, then borrow from it. Use the tone or style of her profile in your own.

After scanning all the other women looking for love, you'll start to get a good idea of what works and what doesn't. Also, don't be afraid to contact other women online and ask them what has and hasn't worked in their hunt for online romance. You can all further one another's cause. If you're worried about "helping the competition," pick women from other parts of the country.

Making the Connection

When He Contacts You

Once someone contacts you, it's time to make an impression that will guide the interaction in a way that saves time and aggravation.

Remember, he is not your new pen pal. You want to learn about him and either drop him or get to a date quickly.

1. Before you consider replying, ask yourself if you liked what he said in his e-mail.

2. Most men won't even read your profile. They'll just look at your picture. These guys are just men being men. To weed out the La-Z-Boy recliners from the good guys, ask them to go back and read your profile, and then ask what it was that they liked about you.

3. E-mail as if you've known him your whole life, but do not make sexual references. When writing and answering e-mails, just write when you feel like it. No need to rush or play games.

4. If you want to, arrange a phone conversation within the first three e-mails. Newbies tend to end up stuck in extended e-mail conversations, so ask sooner rather than later. Have him give you his number, and call from a restricted phone.

5. If the call goes well, arrange for a lunch or coffee date only, making it clear that you have something to do right after. Keep it short and sweet.

When You Contact Him

If you find a guy you like, feel free to contact him via e-mail.

1. Compliment him on something specific in his profile, but keep the first e-mail super short. Praise one of his pictures, his music taste, or something funny he wrote in his profile.

2. When he writes back, ask him how the online dating has been going, implying that you are both in this together.

3. Get some basic safety issues out of the way by asking whether he is married, whether he works, and how long he's been on that particular dating site.

4. Follow steps 2 through 5 in "When He Contacts You."

> Note: If you contact someone once and he doesn't get back to you, then contact him again. Sometimes people get busy and forget. That's the benefit of the Internet: Who cares if your Internet self gets rejected? That said, two strikes and he's out. Next.

Your Safety 'Net

Always lean toward being a bit distrusting. Here's how to work with a safety 'net:

1. Try to get as much personal information out of him as possible, but give very little of your own. Instant-messaging programs make this easier.

2. First meetings should always be in busy public places. When you leave, don't walk directly back to your home.

3. Get his first and last name, and search his identity online.

4. If you can meet him only at night, have him meet you while you're out with girlfriends.

5. Take a little extra time to get to know him before you invite him back to your crib. Make sure that a roommate or neighbor is home for the first visit. He doesn't need to see them, but you're safer with someone else nearby.

6. If you feel any indication that something is "off," then cancel the date/meeting altogether. It's not worth the safety risk. Just say a family emergency arose and you'll get back to him.

This may all sound a bit paranoid, but trust your instincts and have a safe date.

How Guys Operate Online

You should be aware of what you're up against when it comes to how guys view the women of cyberspace.

- Some men think of you as easy targets because you're desperate enough to look for love on the Internet.

- Some men take advantage of the fact that you can't hear their voices or see their eyes, which makes it much easier for them to lie. Remember, any guy can be an Ivy grad online.

- Men often employ a "shotgun" approach by sending out dozens of e-mails to every girl imaginable to see which ones are easiest. These guys are soon sniffed out: Just e-mail them a few random yet specific things about yourself and see if they remember any of the details two or three days later. You can also lie and ask them if they remember your telling them about your aunt from Nebraska. (You don't have an aunt from Nebraska.)

- 'Net cruisers are looking for easy targets and will put in very little effort—unless they find you extremely hot. So make the guy do a bit of work. And if you're hot, know that you'll have to go extra slow with men you meet online.

My parting advice: Always proceed online in the same way you would when meeting someone the old-fashioned way. Pay close attention to how he presents himself, and what words he uses to express his interest. Cut a guy a little slack if he's no Shakespeare, or if he comments on your pictures. React like a woman who's in charge and let him know that you may be single but you're not alone.

Chapter 32

Fly Like an Eagle with a "Wingman"

The expression "I'll just wing it" has solved most of the world's problems. (Say this next part in a soft, suspicious voice.) Wait, maybe winging it is a bad idea when performing medical procedures or packing parachutes or planning a war. Hmmm . . . Come to think of it, it's not great on television, either. Maybe the only place winging it really works is in the domain of relationships.

Find a wingman, or wingwoman, to aid you in meeting and seducing the person of your choice. Going out with a great wingman is the equivalent of loading the deck in your favor. It's cheating, and who doesn't love to cheat: you get a higher score without doing all the work. It's the equivalent of not paying retail.

Let's learn who makes the best wingman.

- The wingman must be in a relationship. If it's a wingwoman, she must not be better looking than you. If it's a wingman, which is preferable, it helps if he's outgoing and funny.

- Your wingperson must understand that this is a serious mission that requires focus.

- In case there are no good boys in the hood, this wingman must be fun to hang with so that the outing isn't a total waste of time.

How to Conquer with Your Wingman

Your wingman's job is to strike up conversations with strangers so that you don't appear desperate. Once the connection has been made, the wingman needs to talk you up, keep the conversation rolling through the awkward stages, and then let you and your target talk. Finally, the wingman is in charge of the exchange of phone numbers or e-mails (if you are too shy) and, regardless of the scenario, the exit plan for you both. And don't forget: you should buy your wingman a drink.

Why It Works

The wingman creates a subtle blend of titillating—I was going to ramble here, but instead I'll say this: two heads are better than one, and the wingman can do the dirty work. Having a wingman takes the pressure off a first hello, and people feel more at ease talking to you when you're with someone. If there are other people standing with your target, the wingman can distract them while you move in for the kill. It really is a relationship made in heaven. I've used the wingwoman strategy so much that it's like shooting fish in a barrel. Trust me, you should try it. If you have tried it and it hasn't worked, then find a new wingman.

Boy Meets Girl

If a relationship were like building a house, dating would be laying the foundation. When girl meets boy and sparks fly, it's time to prepare the groundwork for a future together. The relationship could fail, but if it does work, you want to be ready for it. I recommend going into each relationship open-minded but not blind. To do that, you need to think about how to pour that cement in the smoothest way possible, and make sure it dries without cracking. Now let's get started building . . . er, dating.

Dating on the Clock

When we begin dating you, your figure is not the only hourglass we want to turn upside down. I'll let you in on a secret: we Bad Boys know exactly how many grains of sand will slide through before the end of a relationship. That's right. We've dated and flirted with so many women that we can tell exactly how long the relationship will last—usually within the first fifteen minutes of meeting you. And, believe me, most guys out there have this insight. For example:

- drunk woman in a bar = one or two nights
- woman just out of college = a few months at best
- woman between the ages of twenty-four and twenty-eight = a few weeks to a few months
- divorced or single mom = a few months to several years, depending on her lifestyle
- non-desperate, non–husband hunting woman twenty-eight-plus = open-ended

These may strike you as gross generalizations, and that's good, because they are. But there's some truth here, because *men look at relationships like business transactions.* And *all business transactions have a shelf life.* We look for indications from you that will give our relationship a time-frame potential. I've dated women from all five categories, and without getting into exact numbers, let's just say that I know what I'm talking about.

The clock starts ticking in the first few minutes. Just as you're evaluating your man, he's evaluating you and attempting to see a possible future. But there's a key difference: guys are plotting a way to stay with you long enough to have sex, even if they don't like you or plan on having anything more than a booty call. I'm sure you knew that. Although we pigeonhole women into categories, every single woman is potentially "bed-able."

The Categories

- Keepers (sexy and fun)
- Meet the parents
- Random sex partner/on-again-off-again relationship
- One-to-three-month fake girlfriend
- What was I thinking?
- Close my eyes and think of Jessica Alba

What We Do to Evaluate You

When I'm dating a new woman, I listen to her and try to gauge how easy it will be for me to run the relationship. It's not that I want to run the relationship. I want someone who is challenging and spontaneous. So, the easier I think it would be for me to run the relationship, the sooner I will get bored, and the shorter our relationship will be. I can literally put a mental time limit on our relationship from the get-go, and know when—and how—it's going to end.

This may seem basic, yet women frequently never see the end coming. You know all your girlfriends who were dumped seemingly for no reason? This is why. They ran out the clock. In my case, I wouldn't have been in nearly so many drive-thru relationships if women had known about the clock and had planned ahead.

What You Should Do

There's an easy way to turn off your man's dating clock: simply never let a single pattern or stereotype be revealed in what you say, how you say it, how you dress, or what you demonstratively expect from the guy. *Consistent spontaneity.* Keep him guessing. Outsmart him. Use everything I've told you in this book to shatter his hourglass into a million pieces. You can do it. He'll be sitting there looking at you, silently determining your expiration date, when all of a sudden you'll throw him for a loop. You'll say something or do something that causes cognitive dissonance. For example, you could blurt out, "I've always wondered why men are into seeing two women together" or "I never get wild until I'm with someone for a while." Saying things like this plays right into his "wish list." Such comments are specific enough to get him thinking, but not so concrete that they signify that you'll deliver. Now he has to go back to square one. It's not a game; it's just being smart.

I love when a woman surprises me. I love it when a woman I thought was a "Where is this relationship going?" type turns out to be super cool and confident. I also love it when I think a woman is easy, and it turns out that *she's* using *me.* These are the women who get the best men, and every single one of you has the potential to be that woman. Men like a good surprise, always.

Recently I was dating a girl named Amy . . . okay, I was dating seventeen girls, and Amy was one of them. I put Amy in the "take her to dinner, fool around, and let it fizzle" category. Surprisingly, she turned out to be her own person and an amazing kisser, and totally won me over with her sexy independence. Amy called me when she felt like it. She saw me consistently but randomly. She didn't play games, and she had a life outside of our relationship, which made me feel both unfettered but also challenged by the fact that she could definitely live without me. I stopped dating the other seventeen and focused on her, because she stopped the clock!

Chapter 34

The Anti-Date

Do I have spinach in my teeth? Do I look okay? Does he think I'm hot? Dates are stressful—so stressful that when we date, most of our attention is focused on ourselves. What does that mean? It means we're not paying attention to the other person. Why does that matter? Because on a first date, people reveal themselves. The information you can gather on a first date is priceless; it can either signal a great match or save you from unnecessary heartache down the road. But we tend to waste this opportunity, instead spending the first date focusing on ourselves, wasting hours of time that could be spent making a decision.

You can just stop worrying about yourself. I am about to explode your dating world, and tell you that there's an easier way. From now on, you don't need to put yourself through the hells of early dating. Allow me to introduce the anti-date.

Notice that *anti-date* sounds a lot like *antidote*. The anti-date is an antidote to everything that is wrong with first dates: nerves, discomfort, pressure, and self-consciousness. It's your little purple pill. A first date should be nothing more than a meet-and-greet. You're both interested in each other, yet no one is making plans to go ring shopping. We all want the first date to go well and lead to a second, third, and tenth date. That's where the anti-date comes in.

Anti-Date (n.) A datelike scenario where both parties are interested in each other but haven't yet committed to the words "I like you." They intelligently decide to keep a first meeting short, sweet, and friendly. One of the two people has made a concerted effort to stress the fact that his/her interest is potentially romantic (we're talking more than buddies), but the meeting remains casual.

If you have trouble letting the other person know that you could think of them as dateable, you can do two things: (1) flirt by complimenting him/her on something physical, or (2) tell him/her point blank that you don't think of him/her as a brother/sister. You are attracted.

How to Conduct an Anti-Date

When a guy asks you out—or you ask him out—simply pick a short outing (say sixty minutes). Examples include a walk in the park, a coffee, or lunch. Make sure you have plans right after—you want to leave the party while you're still having a good time, so he wants more of you. It's best to have anti-dates in the daytime or, if your schedule won't allow, as a quick drink after work.

Next, verbally acknowledge that this is a "get-together" intended to allow you to get to know him. If you want to be really strict about this, offer to go dutch. Offering to go dutch tells a guy that you're independent and weren't pretending to want "just a get-together." Instead, you're sending the message that you mean business and you're taking charge. However, I would recommend that if he offers, let him pay; there are some things even the anti-date shouldn't mess with.

Once on the anti-date, forget about *you* and pay strict attention to *him*. Really listen. He'll give you tons of information in this first hour. Glance in a mirror before you meet him, check your clothes and makeup, and then drop your self-awareness. This is the time to engage him in lighthearted conversation that stimulates his opinion muscle; you want to hear his take on things. I've said this before. Hearing a man's perceptions and getting a take on his sense of humor will tell you more about him than having him recite a résumé of where he's from, what college he went to, and what his ethnic background is. I recommend discussions on music, traveling, real estate, and education. Pick something specific and see how he feels about it. Let the conversation flow in whatever direction it wants to take, but keep it fun.

Ending the Anti-Date

There are three ways you can end an anti-date, with each one depending on your gut instinct:

1. If you're undecided, tell him you thought it was fun and that he should call you so you can have "lunch" again sometime soon. You're setting up a second anti-date.

2. If you hate him and want him to crawl back into the river slime from which he came . . . okay, maybe that's a little harsh. Let's just say you didn't hit it off. Be polite and thank him for meeting with you. No need to say, "I'll talk to you soon."

3. If you like him, leave him with a sexy sign-off: a naughty smile, a few choice words (e.g., "I was going to fold socks before bed tonight but now I'm distracted"), an extended hug, or a flash of cleavage or leg. (You know how to do that without seeming obvious.)

The anti-date works. When I have told women that we were going on an anti-date, at first they were visibly confused, but once I explained what it was and why I wanted to date like this, they were relieved and enjoyed it—as well as the romantic dates that followed.

The biggest difference between the anti-date and the one that follows is that on the next date, you have both silently agreed that you're definitely interested. The mood of the first true romantic encounter will then feel heightened.

Chapter 35

Right Place, Right Time

Location, location, location isn't just a byword for real estate. Location can greatly affect how two people interact, and can, therefore, affect the outcome of a date. If the location is too noisy, you can't hear each other ("What's that, you like doggy sex?" "No, I said I have a dog named Rex"). If there are too many other couples, then you feel as if you're speed-dating. If you're in a place with ambiance that is more romantic than the current level of the relationship, it's just awkward. So choose carefully.

Ask yourself some questions: Where are you most happy and comfortable? At what social place do you have the most fun? This is the place where you should have your dates! Not at a formal restaurant where you just wanna put on something more comfortable and sit Indian-style, or in a dive bar that makes you want to go take a shower. *Have dates where you are comfortable.*

What Not to Do

Not too long ago I went out with this idiot—or maybe I was the idiot for dating her (that sounds more like it)—who thought nothing of requesting we go to a restaurant that she had frequented with her ex. We bickered a lot in general as a couple, and because her request was a mild infraction in comparison with the others she committed, I let it slide, and visited her favorite sushi place with her. You can guess what this place did to our relationship. The restaurant made her remember how much she loved her ex, and eventually she returned to him. So, ultimately, I was the stupid one. The point? Don't go to places you used to go to with someone else.

The Problem and the Fix

Here's the problem: Any man worth his salt is going to pick a place where the two of you can get to know each other, which will most likely be either a bar or restaurant. Most times you might not have much say in where to go. The good news is that it's totally appropriate to make suggestions on the mood and tempo surrounding the eating and drinking. If he's hell-bent on a particular place, then go online and check it out or ask around. If it's someplace you think you'll hate, politely ask if the two of you can go there on another night, while offering a selection of alternatives. Let him pick so he feels that it's his decision.

Great Date Locations

In the City

Pick restaurants or bars where the vibe is relaxed. Avoid expensive or overly trendy hotspots. You're aiming for a place with good food, good service, reasonable prices, low-level noise, and people like you two.

In the Suburbs

In the 'burbs, you may want to take your own car. This will depend on how well you know him and if you plan on drinking. (Remember, you shouldn't be drinking too much anyway, especially on a date.) Try to go someplace you both know but frequent rarely—keeping in mind that depending on your choice, the whole town may know about your date. Or pick a place you've both only heard of but would like to try together. This could become "your place," if things work out.

In the Country

Rural communities are tough. I lived in Vermont for a long time, and I can tell you that your choice of restaurants and hangouts isn't broad. You'll know everyone in the place, and if you don't like them, you'll lack other options, because most mom-and-pop places are quite limited in ambiance. The solution? Cook for each other. That's right, Betty Crocker. Get out the pots and pans and cook up a storm—or have him cook up a storm. Some points to remember:

- You are going to be in the comfort of your home or he'll be in the comfort of his, but this does not mean sex should be on the dessert menu. Treat the date as if you were at a restaurant.

- Make something you've made before, and don't make too much of it.

- Don't make anything that gives you gas or bad breath.

- If you cook, he brings the wine; if he cooks, you do.

- If it's a first "cook over," clean up when the other person has gone. Otherwise it's nice to help each other.

Lots of women say they're more comfortable on their own turf, so clean up that pit you call a castle and invite him into your comfort zone: your home, sweet home.

Bonus Ideas

The following is a list of ideas you may not have considered for a fun date.

- **Biking.** It's easy, and if you don't own a bike, chances are you'll find a rental place in your neck of the woods.
- **Fishing.** Guys are happy to help with the worm. Bring food for a picnic.

- **Hiking.** Have "theme" conversations. Come up with and sing silly songs. Play the dictionary game where you try to stump him with vocabulary. Identify your favorite tree. Or play "I Spy" as you walk along. Keep the hike to around an hour.
- **Bowling and playing pool.** There's a reason why couples bond in lanes and bars.
- **Pottery making.** Go to one of those do-it-yourself pottery places and paint plates together.
- **Playing Operation.** The children's game. It's quite fun.
- **Going to comedy clubs.** Ha-ha.
- **Enjoying karaoke night.** *And IIIIIIII will always love yoouuuuuu.*

The more truthful you are with yourself about when and where you are the happiest and the most comfortable, the better chance you have of making a love connection. Go for something similar in flavor to what you're used to, but different enough that it's exciting.

Chapter 36

Head Games

One of the most common questions I hear is, "When should I call, text, or e-mail a person after a date?"

I am reminded of the movie theater: silence is golden. What's the point? Not calling or not saying anything at all can speak volumes and is, most often, your best choice.

Silence *is* doing something. People think that action requires movement—and, yes, sometimes it does. However, being quiet can be more effective than the loudest drum. Why? Well, think about it. Most of us don't sit home and think about how much a person is crazy in love with us. Just the opposite: we sit around and dwell on what we may have done that they didn't like, and play out potential relationship scenarios in our heads. It's a form of masochism. Use this basic fact to your advantage in the dating world.

Being quiet gives you options. Yes, this technique is a head game. However, by being quiet, you let the other person cook a little. You're giving them the time to play out scenarios of their own (why deprive them of such pleasure?), while keeping them on their toes, and you appear confident and spontaneous. Plus, it gives the guy the time to break down and call you. All wonderful things in a relationship.

Silence Is Golden

Silence is golden whenever:

- you are indecisive about whether or not to call;

- you didn't get the vibe that he liked you that much;
- he just pissed you off; or
- he rudely broke up with you.

Overthinking things is the root of all evil in relationships. Women like to engage in overthinking at every opportunity. But this is particularly a killer when it comes to relationships, because you'll often act as if certain fantasy scenarios were real. This can get you in trouble and make you angst-ridden. It also leads to insecure phone calls and long-winded e-mails. Bite your tongue.

How to Be Silent

Stop and think about what silence does to you, and realize that it does the same thing to men. You want to be the silent giver, not the silent sufferer. The best way to do that is to bite the bullet and just not call until you have let some time pass and can feel confident when you send out that e-mail or dial that number. Wait until you feel the "I don't really care what the outcome is" feeling. When you honestly feel that inside yourself, it's time to break the silence.

Note: This does not include calling to vent or get closure from someone who has rudely broken up with you. Those people are to be left in the dirty dust they call their lives. Those people are dead to you and should never be called again. Don't worry, as time passes you'll be thrilled you never rang them. Trust me, it will eat away at them.

Confidence in Silence

Silence builds confidence. At times, we are desperate to know whether we're wanted, even if for no other reason than curiosity. By

allowing yourself to be silent and not make rash relationship decisions or become angst-ridden, you are showing that you have confidence in yourself, and faith that you are such a wonderful woman
that all the chips will fall comfortably where they may. You trust
yourself and have confidence.

It Ain't Easy

The truth is, being silent when you want to call is *really* tough.
When you're staring at the phone and thinking about how much
you want to hear his voice on the other end, make yourself get up
and go outside for a half hour. Force yourself. Don't touch that
phone! Bottom line: *Shhhhh.*

Chapter 37

Tic-Tac-Yo

Life is full of games. From Xbox to rock-paper-scissors, we play games all the time. What makes you think that games would stop in matters of the heart? They don't.

Even though we all say that we hate playing games, we all do it. What we really hate are boring games, bad players, or, worse, losing. The toughest thing about the dating game is that the rules are foggy at best and, truth be told, the question of who wins is somewhat subjective. But we all know what it feels like to lose. So let's not do that anymore. I'm going to show you how to give yourself the best chance at winning.

Games in Nature

To truly understand how to be an effective player in the dating game, you have to look to nature. In the animal kingdom, various species have developed some very clever ways of courting: a doe will pace for weeks to tease a buck, salmon will swim thousands of miles to spawn and die, and penguins will stand in the freezing cold for months. My point? We're no different. Our mating rituals are just as wacky. And just as predictable. Humans happen to produce a number of predictable—and even ingrained—responses to all sorts of stimulus. I'm going to teach you how to use games purposely to provoke the predictable reactions that will work in your favor. From this sentence on, we're going to stop questioning the game and instead embrace it—and then win it! Let's play ball.

The Game Plan: Playing to Win

Here's your game plan of five strategies for winning and coming out on top—pun intended. The trick is to mix in so many game techniques that he becomes dumbfounded, and then becomes your puppet. If he's smart and tough, he'll be a worthy opponent and you two will have a blast. The thing to remember is to have fun and think of it as a game when you're in the middle of it. That won't always be easy. But the good news is that occasionally nature throws us a bone of simplicity. Sometimes everything is just *right*, and you don't need too many checks and balances. In the meantime, however, you have to keep your self-esteem intact and your game face on, so listen up. Your strategies are:

- unpredictability and spontaneity;
- creating rules for the sole purpose of breaking them;
- not calling;
- using sexy words; and
- deploying sex as a weapon—sometimes.

Unpredictability and Spontaneity

One thing is for sure: human beings are curious. Take advantage of that by keeping your man off guard, off balance, and always wondering. The best way to do this is as follows:

1. Always dress sexy, but never in the same style. If you wear a miniskirt one day, go with tomboy cute the next day and professionally sexy on the third day.

2. Never call, e-mail, or text him in any predictable way. This means that you should call whenever you want to call (within reason) or not at all. Vary the time of day. Say, for example, you would normally call right after work if you got a message from him. Instead, call him during the day or early the next morning.

Juggle it around a bit; never let him be able to "expect" your call. He calls, you text. He e-mails, you call. He texts, you e-mail two days later. You may even choose not to call at all. This inconsistency is deadly in a good way.

3. Be on time for dates and cancel occasionally. Being on time is unusual when it comes to women (sorry, but it's true), so this will set you apart and get him thinking. And cancel once in a while. The best way to cancel for the most effect is by arranging something for a night when you already have plans to do something else (he doesn't know this), and then apologize and cancel. Keep in mind that you don't want to be rude and cancel at the last minute: Cancel the night before or very early in the morning. Do this by phone; do not text or e-mail! Calling shows that you have balls.

4. If you're not naughty by nature, then blurt out some sort of profanity or outrageous comment. Don't go overboard. Just make it noticeably racier than usual.

5. Invite him out. Ask him on a date. If he says no, just shrug it off and don't return his calls for a few days. You want to get this tiger to jump through hoops for you, so you have to be very proactive here.

Overall, you don't want to let your man/victim be able to sense any patterns about you, because if he does, he'll quickly settle in around those patterns—and then lose interest. In other words, you want to keep him from figuring you out for as long as possible. It's consistent spontaneity, as I've mentioned before.

Creating Rules for Breaking

Hypocrisy upsets men as much as women; double standards are a hot point for all of us. Yet if you exercise hypocrisy in the right way, it will get your man on the warpath, where he is actively seeking to understand how you can get away with something. You provoke this by creating rules that you know are okay for women to break, but not for guys.

- Make a rule that he can't use his phone at the table while you're eating. Then, when your phone rings, answer it, but keep the conversation super brief. If he questions the hypocrisy, just answer, "Girls talk on the phone more than guys. We can't help it, sorry. I won't do it again."

- Say that you don't really like kissing in public, and then plant one on him. Tell him you couldn't help yourself.

- Have him help you lift something in your home because you can't lift it. Then bring up how strong you feel from going to the gym.

Employing hypocrisy as one of your subtler strategies can throw off his game plan. It works because in the arena of romance, it's okay not to play fair sometimes. (Men don't always play fair, so why should you?) This is "hypocritical hardball," and it just may be the thing that keeps you from being banished to left field.

Keep in mind, though, that these "rules for breaking" are cute and fun, and much different from the standards and boundaries you lay down for your relationship (see Chapter 45). Make sure he can tell the difference. Also, you want to use the "good for girls, not good for guys" thing sparingly, as you don't want him to get so angry that he drops you.

Not Calling

I start this section with a warning: Keep in mind that he may "not call" you, too. Calling is a two-way street, and you don't want to let this strategy backfire. If you find he is not calling when he said he would, or is obviously following the three-day rule or another strategy, then beat him at his own game by referring back to the ideas under "Unpredictability." (Guys love to hate this.) Or try these strategies:

1. Don't call for a day after he's left a message.

2. Don't call him if he text-messages you and asks you to call. And don't text him back, either.

3. If he calls you and you're "busy" or on the phone, call him back at a random time and date.

4. Refer to number 2 under "Unpredictability and Spontaneity."

Just like everything else I'm teaching you, use "not calling" sparingly—just enough to keep him on his toes.

Using Sexy Words

The words you use are as important as what you talk about. For example, in a political discussion, you might mix strong, opinionated words with more playful choices. One great strategy to keep relations calm is to direct your vehemence at the conversation topic, not at him. However, the most powerful way to use words is sexually. There are a handful of words that, when falling from a woman's lips, drive men crazy.

- Panties
- Thong
- Sex
- Tits
- Ass
- _____ [Any word describing sex or a woman's body or undergarments will suffice here.]

By sprinkling your conversation with these words, you make his mind drift onto sexual topics. You are controlling his thoughts, which of course gives you the edge.

Deploying Sex as a Weapon

Using sex as a weapon can prove to be a double-edged sword. Consider yourself warned. If you are going to use the "promise of sexual intimacy" as a carrot on a string, then, on occasion, you'll have to deliver. Here is the way you do it without painting yourself into a sexual corner, appearing to be a tease, or becoming the object of a grudge:

- Be sexually flirtatious, but not *too* flirtatious. Thumbs-down include flashing him, overtly touching him, or promising anything explicit.

- If you are ready to have sex, then do so on your terms.

- If he upsets you or hasn't been attentive, tell him that you need to be in the mood, and that because of his rude actions you are not in the mood. No need to take one for the team here. Reschedule your session.

- Be intimate at unexpected moments and in unexpected locations.

Q&A

Q: I don't like playing games. Why should I follow this advice, since it seems like a lot of game-playing?

A: Games are fun. If it doesn't feel fun, then chances are you're not playing correctly, or you're playing with someone who cheats. You need to find someone with whom you enjoy playing the game—and then relax and have *fun*.

The trick to playing—and winning—the game is paying attention and understanding human nature. Listen carefully to the guy you're with; he'll tell you everything you need to know. Look at how he dresses, what he watches on TV, what he talks about. Try to know him inside and out. Give as little info about yourself as possible while in turn learning more about him than his own mother. Then use this info to strategize. There is very little reason to be destructive . . . so don't be. It's a game, and the overtone should always be a wink and a smirk, signaling that you are just having fun.

As with any game, practice makes perfect. There will be moments of intrigue, angst, and second-guessing, but when you get better, you'll start to see it for what it is: exhilarating!

Chapter 38

Sext Messaging

Text messaging, or as I like to refer to it, "sext messaging," is not just a fad. It's the biggest form of foreplay since kissing. Here we're going to talk about text messaging as a tool in seduction and baiting. I'll also fill you in on if and when to send naughty pictures.

Foreplay

Words are powerful, and if you choose the right ones at the right time, they can have a tantalizing effect. Want to whip your man into a frenzy of arousal? Keep your messages short and sweet, choose phrases that are more suggestive than overt, and always remember that he may not be the only one who reads them . . . that should save you some carpal tunnel problems. I know your thumbs are wanting to click away frenetically on that little cell phone keypad, but with texting, less is more. On that note, here are some great examples of text messages I've received that were highly effective at increasing my interest in the sender:

- "I woke up thinking about you . . . mmmm."
- "I have something I want to show you ;-)"
- "It's hard to text with just one hand . . . hee hee."
- "I love the way you feel."
- "Thank you."

Naughty little messages received while your man's at work or out with the guys can get his wheels spinning in your direction. Receiving sext messages is also extremely intimate, because the whole exchange happens internally: he's not reading it aloud, so you're literally getting inside his head! Think about that the next time your thumbs are dancing away on the keypad.

Sexting Images

Seducing with sext messages is a skill that requires knowing your man and defining the personal boundaries you are comfortable with. I've already explained that using the right words can be a powerful stimulator; add the right picture, and you're deadly. But if you do choose to send pictures, try to get him to send an incriminating photo of himself first. Never hurts to have collateral!

- Send photos only after you trust him.

- Pictures are best delivered with comedic captions; sex and comedy are a man's favorite pastime.

- Never include your face or any distinguishing details, such as tattoos, identifiable locations or objects in the background, or jewelry.

- Raunchy is not usually the best choice, but nudity in small doses is hot. For example, try a head-on shot with your arms pushing your chest together. You could also get a shot of your bum at a three-quarter angle, a close-up of your lips, or a lingerie picture. In general, a close-up of any provocative body part does the job.

- In general, women dating younger men (sixteen to thirty-two) should not send photos that they wouldn't want the entire world to see. In other words, make sure your guy is mature enough not to show all his buddies, but assume he's going to show at least one friend.

• Explain that any exploitation of your personal sext messages is a deal breaker, and that he'll be walkin' if he breaks this code of trust.

Baiting

Sext messaging can also be used to bait someone. This takes a certain amount of creativity and storytelling skill. I call this the "I know something you don't know" philosophy. It's sophomoric, but it works. Here's how you do it:

1. Think of a sexy story and/or fantasy.

2. Dole out the story in small parts via text. Start by sending a text message that says something like "I've got to tell you something." Just leave it at that, and he'll respond with "What?"

3. You respond with "I'll text you in a minute." The point is to get him interested in something you have to say, to slowly bait him into playing along.

4. Chances are he'll call you and ask you to explain verbally. This you must resist. Don't pick up the phone.

5. Once you have him hooked, text the fantasy in small, three- to ten-word bits. He'll respond like one of Pavlov's dogs.

The more creative you are, the more fun you'll have. You'll also have a chance to exercise the power of leading him around. It's a win-win situation.

Why Men Use Text Messaging

Most men use texting as a weapon in their dating arsenal. Here's why:

- We can text from just about anywhere, such as while we're on a date and the girl is in the ladies' room, while we're at work, or while we're sitting on the couch watching the game.

- It's sneaky, and guys love sneaky.

- It doesn't require talking on the phone.

- It makes it easier to lie.

- There is no background noise or anything else that would indicate where we are.

- We can easily keep in touch with up to ten different women (maybe more, if we type fast!).

- Booty texting avoids the risk of rejection over the phone.

- We love having pictures of you naked on our phones. This works mostly in your favor. In sight, in mind.

Texting Isn't a Replacement for Talking

Worried that your man only texts you? Make sure you have him trained to call and communicate in person right from the beginning of the relationship. You do this by being consistent. (I know you want to start being consistently unpredictable, but this is one of those times when playing by the rules works best.) Consistent means that you've told him from the beginning that texting is fine but at least one phone call a day is more appreciated. Compliment him when he calls, and don't text back when he hasn't called. In other words, train him to call you. Making the right call on calling and/or texting usually depends on the scenario. I'm giving you guidelines to fall back on when you're not sure, but in general, trust your instincts. If you don't have a rule of thumb in place, things can get out of hand down the road. I've had "text wars" with a girlfriend, and I've heard of guys breaking up via text. I made the mistake of letting one girl text so much that when she dumped me, she felt it was appropriate that she do so over the phone instead of face to face. Lesson learned. Texting should be used to enhance seduction, not as a surrogate form of human interaction!

These days, we are communicating more often but saying less. Rapid communication isn't always good communication. As long as human beings have blood in their veins and air in their lungs, there will be no replacement for human contact.

Chapter 39

Tough Call

Nature weeds out the weak birds, plants, and insects by allowing only the strong—and smart—to survive. Men and women do the same thing to each other, with each forcing the other to survive through a series of relationship tests. Just like the squirrel that misjudges a branch-to-branch leap is a goner, the guy who ignores your emotional signals is also a goner.

Although these tests don't have life-and-death consequences, they're still important. In most relationships, the female tests the male to see if he's alpha enough, yet still sensitive to her needs.

However, Bad Boys and edgy men will sometimes turn the tables and test you. I know you find this annoying, so I'll explain why and how we do it so you can know how to respond. First up: Why do we do this?

- we've become so skilled at winning women we're looking for a challenge;
- people are much more likely to show their true colors when pissed off; and
- we want a fast way to see where your strengths and weaknesses lie.

Have you ever been with a guy who suddenly seems intentionally adversarial in a conversation, pushing your buttons (albeit never physically)? He's testing you. His dialogue will have a playful tone, but with a serious undercurrent. (You'll know he's not testing you when he agrees with you often and is extremely selective in the battles he chooses.)

When Bad Boys Are Testing You

Most Bad Boys will push your buttons on purpose in the following four scenarios:

1. When We Sense a Woman Is Not Strong Enough to Deal with Us

If I meet a woman who seems like she might easily cave under normal relationship and life stress, I will intentionally see how far I can push her to see what her breaking point is. I'm not doing this to be mean. Quite the contrary: I want to know early on if we're fundamentally not a good match. I don't want to hurt her. Therefore, if she is too easily pushed around, I will confirm that and then find the exit very quickly. For example, I may begin a discussion on a topic she knows a lot about, and then play devil's advocate. I want to see if she'll stand up to me and stand up for herself.

I once had a talk with a girl I was dating about the value of personality versus skills in the workplace. I knew she was going to say skills were more important to overall success. The argument ignited as planned, and within moments she grew silent with frustration. Upon seeing this, I yelled, "God, stick up for yourself! Tell me to shut the hell up! Don't get quiet!" This two-minute conversation reminded me that I love verbal women, and that she and I weren't a great match.

2. When a Woman Is a Bitch

Bitchy women tend to carry themselves with a sense of calm entitlement. They have an "it's my way or the highway" attitude. They rarely trip or even stumble when calm. But if you piss them off, the mistakes will fly out like wood from a chipper, and while they are spewing, they will reveal their weaknesses. I take note of everything, and before you know it, their highway is going my way. Even the toughest shells have nuts inside. I've cracked a few; I should know. Of course, through all of the yelling, I will never reveal what signs I'm listening for. In the heat of the moment, bitchy women have called me another guy's name, run down a list of things they hate about me, and outlined, in detail, everything I've ever done that made them feel like less than a "princess." My job is to listen, take it all in, and plan my response—a response that can take weeks, and sometimes will arrive in the form of revenge, depending on how mean-spirited the woman was in her outburst.

3. When a Woman Is Too Quiet

A woman is noticeably quiet around a man for one of three reasons:

1. she's shy;
2. she's brilliant; or
3. she's opinionless.

Of course, before we can have a relationship, I need to know which it is. And I'm going to figure it out by ruffling some feathers. It works like a charm—her response gives everything away. Remember: *anger* and *alcohol* both begin with the letter *a*, and they are both the best truth serums around.

I recently went out with a fairly conservative woman who, I'm pretty sure, graduated with honors from etiquette class. The only way I could get Sophie to open up about her feelings was to pour her more wine or enrage her. I eventually got to the bottom of who she was, and that's what I wanted. She turned out to be an amazing woman, and we're still friends. My point is that I—and most Bad Boys—will use whatever strategies are necessary to get someone to speak from the heart and act uninhibited.

Strong, quiet women can be extremely sexy—particularly if they remain quiet at my ruffling attempts, and respond with a few choice words. Then I'm beaten at my own game.

4. When We're Trying to Heat Things Up Sexually

Makeup sex is a cliché, and it's a cliché for a reason: it works. I apologize for admitting this, but I've met women who feel safe being naughty only after a heated discussion or fight. On occasion, I will pick a fight simply to ensure that the makeup sex will be rough and ready. Okay, so I'm not really sorry.

Chapter 40

Naughty by Nature

It is my firm belief that women want to be just as naughty as men. However, society says that a woman shouldn't let go. It's a big no-no. So she needs an "excuse" to be naughty, while a man just needs a "place." It's the man's job to give you whatever "excuse" you need to let yourself go. But how can we play if everyone is judging us?

There are four unwritten "rules" that we all tacitly abide by (there are more, but these are the most important, and why bore you with the rules you're already aware of?):

1. Women are not supposed to sleep with a man on the first date.
2. Women are not supposed to be overtly sexual in the way they speak or act.
3. Men make the first move.
4. Women coyly resist our early advances. (No, I am not talking about actual resistance, which we respect!)

These social guidelines create a problem for men: How do we get you to break all those commandments without making you feel cheap or easy? We have to help you "check off" the rules one by one so that you can feel good about being bad.

In rides the use of comedy.

Comedy and charm are the two best elixirs when it comes to putting those stupid rules to rest. Thus the phrase "charming the pants off you."

Although dating and romance are supposed to be fun, they're often filled with angst—that is, until a man who is confident, funny, and charming waltzes into a woman's life, at which point she suddenly views the rules as what they are: silly. The angst is gone. She is much more apt to be free, let her hair down, and not care what anyone thinks; she can safely be her naughty self. By keeping things light and fun, we've created an environment that is safe. Have you ever seen those inflatable fun houses that children bounce around in unharmed? That's our goal. We want you to feel happy and safe enough to take your shoes off and jump around. Ah, now we're getting somewhere.

How Bad Boys Get You to Scrap the Rules

I'll give you two examples of exactly how I do this, so you know what to look for.

1. The Debbie Date

The first thing I do is pick a place that is not too noisy and not too quiet, because I want us to feel like two friends going out to have fun. Next, I make sure we can both have a drink, though that's not mandatory. Now comes the eye-to-eye conversation across the table. This is a no-holds-barred gabbing session about work, family, activities, and music. All of which is continually sprinkled with compliments and soft sexual connotations. Something like this:

> STEVE: Debbie, what's the farthest you've ever walked?
> DEBBIE: I don't know, that's an odd question. Maybe five miles.
> STEVE: How about carried?
> DEBBIE: What do you mean carried?
> STEVE: Like, if I were to pick you up right now, throw you over my shoulder, and carry you home, how far would we have to go to break your old record?

STEVE AND DEBBIE: [Laugh]

DEBBIE: Oh, about ten miles.

STEVE: Well, I'll finish eating, and then we'd better get going. Don't worry, I'll hold your skirt down so no one gets a peek.

DEBBIE: That's good, because I never wear undies . . . kidding.

[Debbie could also answer, "Gee, thanks, you're so chivalrous." But the first, flirty answer is preferable.]

STEVE: Do you like to exercise? You look amazing.

Pay careful attention, because it's hard to track these conversations when you're actually in them: The conversation starts with a strange question to pique your interest, and eventually reverts back to the serious topic of exercise. All of this is done in less than thirty seconds. Imagine what can be accomplished in an hour!

The point is that if you're having fun and laughing, it's great for both of you. Just keep your wits about you. Make sure that you excuse yourself, go to the bathroom, wipe off the runny mascara, and think about whether or not this man has other qualities you're truly interested in. If he is joking around too much, bring him back to earth and make him be serious.

Remember, laughing all the way to bed is more common than laughing all the way to the bank! I never see people laughing in a bank. Do you?

2. The Allison Date

By the second half of the date, if the guy is doing a good job, you'll say things like "I can't believe I'm telling you these things." But you're smiling. Why are you saying these things? Because your man has brought up topics that you don't usually talk about honestly.

I've launched conversations on topics ranging from the longest battery life for a vibrator to sex on the beach (which, with all that sand, can be like putting your penis in a pencil sharpener).

This is how I and a lot of other Bad Boys approach the topic of sex: head on.

Let's call this the Allison Date (things are over between me and Debbie, hee hee):

> STEVE: Allison, I'm not being a perv, but I was watching this thing on the Discovery Channel about masturbation, and they said that women do it as much as men, but don't admit it. Why is that? What's the big deal?
>
> ALLISON: I don't know. [Allison is not yet comfortable with the topic.]
>
> STEVE: Oh Allison, let's just talk like adults. Pretend you and I are doctors or something, because this fascinates me. Do you ever "play the banjo"?
>
> ALLISON: [Laughs] Play the banjo? Yes, sometimes.
>
> STEVE: Do you use your hand or a vibrator?
>
> ALLISON: Depends.
>
> STEVE: That noise would bother me if I were a girl . . . especially the gas-powered ones. [I mime starting a chain saw and continue with the sound effects.]
>
> ALLISON: [Laughs]
>
> STEVE: The other thing I don't get is why people want to have sex in a dirty airplane bathroom.
>
> ALLISON: Yeah, I don't get that, either. I would have to be on a very long flight and be very bored.
>
> STEVE: You and I should go to Bora Bora.
>
> ALLISON: I'm in! [Laughs]

We all want to have fun. We all have questions about sex. Many men, myself included, use these truths to further our cause. That cause is seduction. Smart women play along and guide the conversation in a way that is fitting for a lady but also fun for a guy—too much on either side ruins the effect. Smart women also use these conversations to read exactly what their date has in mind for the rest of the evening—which in this case is a lot of tangoing.

How to Behave While Being Naughty

1. Have fun and play along, because men love a certain amount of silliness.
2. Always maintain a bit of feminine decorum; don't get too crude.
3. Look through the jokes to see what else he has to offer.
4. Trust your instincts, and do things after the date on your own terms.

Chapter 41

Be a Tease

Playfully teasing a guy with sexual flirtation is a clever way to keep him interested and test his prowess. As the Aussies say, *Treat 'em mean, keep 'em keen.*

There's a fine line, however, between teasing and being mean. Men consider it cruel—and bitchy—when a woman leads them on but doesn't "put out." Most men would rather she just say, "No, it's never going to happen." Eventually her strategy will explode in her face, because there will be a guy—I just may know one—who is on to her game, and will rightly dump her after finally seeing some action. It's no different than if a guy strings you along, pretending that one day he'll commit, then instead leaves you hanging. It's not nice, and he, too, will get what he deserves: a ride in the dump truck.

I've met several "teases" along the way, and they were a rude awakening to the ways of some women. To a certain extent, I understand the philosophy. There is a certain amount of teasing/abuse that we all love to endure, and the strategy works. However, it's women like Tiffany who take it too far.

I met Tiffany in Boston and e-mailed her quite often. When we talked on the phone, she would talk dirty, make sexually suggestive comments, and explain how badly she wanted to see me. But we were both busy and talked for about two months before we finally found a mutually free weekend. I didn't feel like flying to Boston, so I offered to pay for her ticket to New York. The night she arrived we went to bed and she began getting very sexually excited and wanted "certain" things. She blatantly led me on—take my word on this one—and then, all of a sudden, once she was happy, she shut down and was finished for the evening. Needless to say, I asked her to leave the next morning. It wasn't that Tiffany didn't want to have sex; it was the way in which she went about it. She was teasing in a very immature and callous way.

It's my belief that if you're beautiful, you should flaunt it, because no one stays that way forever. Just because men are tough, however, doesn't mean that we don't have feelings. And we definitely don't enjoy being "dicked" around.

Adding insult to injury, girls like Tiffany ruin it for the truly good women out there, because when a guy is treated poorly, you can be sure that he'll carry that baggage into the next relationship. Hence the expression "Put out or get out." After all, it's only foolish men who spend time and money on women who have no intention of taking things further. For a while after the "Tiffany Experience," I wouldn't buy dinner for a woman unless she had *shown me* that she really liked me.

How Teasing Should Look

Teasing should be nothing more than flirting on steroids. A pumped-up version of yourself, to get the man all hot and bothered. You should use this sparingly so that you don't back yourself into a corner, and into a situation where your man expects more than you're comfortable offering. Just have fun. Examples of good teasing include lighthearted conversation while spontaneously grabbing his ass, jumping on him, or putting his hand on your chest quickly.

Remember, it's okay to tease a little. But intentionally leading someone on without ever planning to consummate the relationship is a form of lying. Most people don't like liars. I know I don't.

Chapter 42

Second Base

Remember first, second, and third base? I'm not talking about baseball. I'm talking about how far you let a guy go with you. First base is kissing, second base is touching over the clothes, third base is touching under the clothes, and a home run is, well, a home run!

It's easier to go back in time to when things were simpler. Take high school, where a day's education included cheating on a math test, putting a live rat in the teacher's car, and making out with a hot substitute. Wait, that might have been only me . . .

Being a bit "high school" in new relationships is a good thing. It takes the pressure off your sex life and gives you both a path to follow.

Relationship Time Machine

It's easier than you think to return to the days when you had an unwritten schedule of how long it should take to go from base to base. There's no need to pitch the idea of going "high school." Simply walk him to first base, with a potential bonus of making out in the backseat of a car. Then "swing" a little harder on each date, thereby letting him know there's more on deck if he's a star player.

Baseball works in your favor when you keep the ball with your team. Move from base to base at whatever speed you're comfortable with, letting him steal a base here and there to get a little more loving with each date. Meanwhile, you can get to know him better and decide whether to go for the grand slam with bases loaded, or to cut it short and tag him out at second. Either way, you'll always be up to bat.

Okay, I've successfully used more baseball metaphors than was thought humanly possible. On to the details.

Why This Works on Men

Going slowly, one base at a time, works because a man's first introduction to the world of women was carried out under these rules. In a word, he's used to it. It's comforting and reassuring for him; he doesn't get frustrated and leave, nor does he get overzealous and head for home base on the second date. He can see the game plan and will stick to it. Most important, it gives you the time to sort out whether or not he's the kind of guy you want on your team.

I've fallen in love after having sex on a first date; I've also dated women who made me wait, and I don't think the worse or the better of them. It's up to you. The most important and productive thing you can do is to be firm and consistent, thereby letting your man know that you are doing things on your own terms, on your own clock. There are times to be consistent and times to be consistently unpredictable. When it comes to moving from base to base, I recommend the former.

Chapter 43

Resist Arrest

Listen up: A lot of you independent, free-living women are making a major mistake. More and more often, my friends and I come across women who are *too* demonstrative that they want sex, or are *too* available for sex.

This may sound odd, given that most healthy men want sex as often as possible. But if you are *too* available, you take away our simple joy of thinking that we have seduced you. We like to feel that we've worked hard to get away with something. Does that sound bad? Well, it's true. The idea is somewhat ingrained in men that women have sex with us as a favor, and if you just drop your clothes, that's no favor.

Instead, by allowing us to pursue you, you are catering to our atavistic desire to hunt. It's a joy. It's also a game. (Even in long relationships, it's important to keep unpredictable fun built into that romance—see Part V.)

How can you set up a "hunting" scenario? Easy: be seductive in a way that makes *him* pursue *you*, and then reward him when he does. This is the best way to get what you both need.

From the time that boys are small, we learn that being naughty—whether stealing a cookie or a kiss—is something that stimulates great inner happiness. That pleasure doesn't go away with age. Therefore, it helps a woman's cause if she can lead us to believe that we are "getting away" with something and being naughty. Women do this with a simple three-step process: teasing, resisting, and giving in. And it just so happens that the same process can be used to revive a faltering sex life.

The Sexual Dance in Three Steps

Step 1: Teasing

Just like you need to "get into the mood," men need to be enticed well before bedtime. This is particularly true in long-term relationships. Do this by performing the clichéd act of teasing. Examples include:

- Walking to the refrigerator naked.
- Bending from the waist instead of the knees.
- Dressing in a way that is unusually sexually provocative for your wardrobe.
- Slapping his ass or doing something physical that a guy would normally do to a girl.

Step 2: Resisting

Resist him if he tries to return your gestures, but do it in a teasing way.

- If he attempts to kiss or fondle you, feel free to kiss him back and begin moving in a way that is all hot and bothered; then smile and walk away.
- If he is aggressive about it, fight him off in a playful way, but resist arrest; this increases his desire to keep pursuing you.

Step 3: Giving In

When you finally give in, it should make him feel as if he's conquered you. Even if it's just for the first few moments of the session, let him think he's getting away with something. Feel free to jump his bones once things are under way.

The three-step process is not meant to be demeaning to women. It simply plays on a man's natural desire to pursue sex by giving him the opportunity to do so. There are other ways to keep the sex exciting, such as a series of touch-and-go quickies, which can also keep that muscle in good shape. But the three-step process is a tried-and-true one that you can use for any relationship at any stage. If a man doesn't want to have sex with you, try these three steps, and if he still doesn't want to, drop him or get it somewhere else. That's what men do.

Find ways to make him pursue you a little more than you are pursuing him—this will successfully keep him on the prowl.

Chapter 44

Spontaneous Combustion

In the dating jungle, there are many variables that go into a woman's decision about whether to have sex: comfort level, alcohol intake, time and place, love, and many more. And then there's always the worry that sex will change the dynamic. Change is good, but not if it ends a relationship.

I'm going to help you figure out how to identify the right moment to turn that corner, and how to maintain power after the act is finished.

When to Sleep Together

Once upon a time I met a woman, became intimate on the first night, we fell in love, and we lived happily ever after for years to come. The end.

A little simple, yes. The truth is, you need to consider each and every situation by its own "rules of gravity." Meaning: the heavier you feel the situation might be, the slower you should go. If he seems a bit deeper than the average Joe, trust your instincts and take it slow.

It is absolutely your choice when and where to sleep together—but keep him guessing when. Whatever your decision, make sure that it's *your decision*. Do not do anything you feel coerced into doing, because that's a lose-lose situation. Let me explain: In general, men can tell the difference between a woman who is doing something she wants to do, and one who is doing something because she feels intimidated into doing so. Smart women who want healthy, balanced

> Note: The decision is a very personal one, and it's not appropriate for me to tell you exactly when to do it (unless you and I are dating, in which case we should sleep together as soon as possible; I suggest my place).

relationships do things on their terms, which sets boundaries for men and shows us that you're in charge of your own welfare. We like that, we respect that, and we want relationships with women like that.

Warning

Don't confuse your own terms with a set of externally imposed, rigid rules. When I meet a woman who is putting me through her "program" in order to get intimate, I get bored. It's obvious she may not be doing things on my terms, but she certainly isn't doing things on her terms, either. Instead, she's got a set of rules from a third source, like a bad relationship advice book or magazine article, and is performing a routine. It's not who she really is! Ladies, whatever you decide, make it your own decision.

It's not the base-to-base trip that we find aggravating, but *how* you do it, and how it makes us feel. So whether you are taking us along one base at a time or hopping from first to third, back to second with a short stop at home, we have to get the feeling that this is the way you've *chosen* to do things with us, and *not* some test you put every guy through. That's boring and worth ignoring.

A Word on Creepy Crawlies

A doctor friend of mine told me that he thought people's biggest fear was AIDS, and after that everything else was no big deal. From a medical standpoint, he was correct, but from an emotional one, he may have been forgetting something: STDs are a social and psychological nightmare, not to mention physically painful. Imagine meeting the man of your dreams and then having to explain to him that you have a permanent STD. Not so much fun.

In general, you have a right to your privacy and so does he—until you're getting busy together, at which point it's important to spill the beans. And waiting to do the deed can actually work in your favor healthwise, because the longer you know a guy, the better the chance you'll have of him opening up on any creepy crawlies he might have. Likewise, if you have some news you want to share, he'll be more forgiving if he knows you better. Over the years, women have told me things that I've been okay with and close-lipped about (not all people are). Go slow and use protection!

Why, Not When

It's not *when* you sleep with a man that matters the most, but *why*. Only you know why. The reason doesn't have to be anything profound or earth-shattering; it can simply be because you feel like it. But don't let your man catch wind that you are apprehensive. I can love a woman if we sleep together on the first night or the three-hundredth night; it all depends on her attitude and confidence, and the sense I get that this was *her* decision. It's sexy when a woman actively decides to sleep with me. I will always try to sway a woman along the way—it's what Bad Boys do—but be steadfast and stick to your guns. We respect that.

Where to Sleep Together

My place or yours? Ah, a timeless dilemma. Where you first sleep together is not as crucial as you might think, but it *can* have an impact on the relationship. In general, I would go to his place. Why? Because a woman's bed is far more special in a man's mind. You can save your place for when you really start to like him. Plus, it's much better if you get up and leave at the end.

Should I Stay or Should I Go?

I have a general rule of thumb for leaving: Unless it's love, the first couple of times, *you* should leave, and not spend the night. This sets a precedent that you are an independent woman and will sleep beside him only when the two of you are more attached; in other words, act like a guy, and let him know that he's expendable. Guys often silently wonder whether you'll stay: "Will she or won't she? I don't really want her to." After we have sex, a strange calm envelops us and we like to be alone. Not always, but sometimes. That's why you'll find many men not being affectionate after sex.

But as you already know, there are no definite rules in the game of love. Ultimately, you should evaluate the situation and do what's best for you at that particular time. Everything you do must be driven from an inner monologue of "I am a strong, independent woman, and this is what I choose to do regardless of the future romantic outcome."

Away from Home

Choosing where you sleep together can be fun: cheesy hotels, in the great outdoors (bring the wet naps), on your desk at work, in the car. The place you choose, even if you don't go all the way, can be a special memory that you share forever.

When I first moved to New York City, I commuted from Vermont and slept on my friend's couch while I found an apartment. One weekend I met a great girl, and even though we didn't intend to have sex (nor did we), we wanted to sleep beside each other. But how? She had curious roommates, and my borrowed couch wasn't big enough for two. So I phoned my friend Tim to ask if I could stay at his place while he was out of town. He agreed, and I informed Scarlet that we had a place to crash. In retrospect, it was very strange: We didn't know each other well, she didn't know Tim, and neither of us knew the apartment, and yet we were going to sleep there together, for the first time. Recipe for tragedy or comedy. Luckily, it turned out to be comedy. At 3:30 a.m., a drunk couple tried to jam their keys into the front door lock, sounding a lot like angry robbers. Scarlet awoke, sat up, and stared with fear at the front door. I got up, looked through the peephole, and scared off the drunks. We laugh about it to this day—and she swears that I know nothing about finding good places to sleep together. But I consider that first night a success because we still remember it fondly. The point is that where you first sleep together should be fun and memorable if at all possible.

Maintaining Power After the Act

You've done the deed, and are worrying that your relationship is now over. How to prevent that? It's simple. Just don't fall into the pattern of having sex every time you see him. Sometimes you feel like it, sometimes you don't. This way, you'll always keep him guessing and on his toes, also known as keeping him on "his best behavior."

Chapter 45

Laying the Groundwork

Once you begin seeing someone—i.e., regularly making plans and spending time with a partner—you need to start laying a solid foundation for the relationship. The foundation building has to happen at the onset of the relationship, as it can be difficult or impossible to build one later. The first couple of weeks are crucial for setting the standard for how your guy will behave throughout the relationship. New affairs are so busy that it can be hard to make foundations a priority, but the pieces will all fall together if you take the time to be consistent in setting your boundaries for the relationship.

What does this mean? Well, it means that you have to pull your self-esteem together and lay down some reasonable standards by which you will both abide. These rules of engagement will keep the relationship strong and give it the best chance to grow into a deep, lasting one—and a pleasant one. We've all seen the marriage where one person doesn't trust the other, or isn't honest, or acts disrespectfully, and the relationship is sometimes miserable for both partners. Relationships are like houses, and marriages such as these were clearly built on swampland, not firm ground.

Don't Worry, He Won't Leave Because of Your Foundation

I know how it feels to meet someone wonderful after dating a bunch of duds. You don't want to lose that person, and as a result, you do the "eggshell walk." You're anxious in your attempts not to disturb the nest. Bad idea. I'm not suggesting that you become a bull in a china shop, but you should slowly but steadily be firm about the points not up for negotiation in the relationship. You have to be willing to lay down the law without fearing you'll lose the guy.

Every woman must have a set of personal standards that she will not compromise just because she wants love. To quote the Bible (don't worry, I'm wearing rubber boots, so the lightning strike doesn't hurt too much), "What has a man achieved if he gains the whole world but loses himself in the process?" You cannot lose yourself in the process. If you keep the rules simple and hold up your end of the bargain, your love will be stronger in the end. If he bails on you, you've just saved yourself months of heartache. Amen.

The Five Foundations of a Solid Relationship

What's reasonable in terms of laying down the law? Here are the five "must-haves" that build relationships, not walls.

1. Trust
2. Respect
3. Personal space
4. Honesty
5. Quality time

Trust

Trust is the most important thing you can have in any healthy relationship, whether with friends or lovers. Without it, your relationship is meaningless. You build trust by handing it out slowly but consistently—don't back up the dump truck and bury someone with your trust, which inevitably leads to a landslide.

The best way to get a guy to be open with you is by clearly stating that you want both of you to be completely honest in the relationship, yet sensitive toward each other. The caveat here is that you cannot ask him to be honest and then freak out when he tells you something honestly. Expressing your feelings is fine; freaking out is the best way to get him to sneak around, thereby throwing trust out the window. Practice *responding*, not *reacting* to each other. Think about the difference.

I often hear stories about partners snooping in each other's e-mail and text messages in an effort to find evidence of cheating. If your relationship boils down to that kind of behavior, it's a sign that things aren't working and you need to move on. Just trust your instincts. It's better to fly the coop than to snoop.

Respect

What is respect? It's fundamentally valuing a person and his needs, wants, and opinions. Teasing and playful ribbing are one thing, but disrespectful behavior, ranging from name-calling to treating someone cruelly, is not acceptable. I guarantee that any little signs of disrespect will escalate and eventually blow up in your face. Avoid name-calling like the plague, and never accept "pet names" that include "Bitch," "Hey, you," or "Ass." Nip that in the bud immediately.

Personal Space

Make it very clear that you have friends and activities that won't always include him, and that you intend to maintain them. At the same time, respect his need for personal space and get to know *his* friends and passions in a nonobtrusive way. By setting up this understanding from the very beginning, there won't be any unwelcome surprises down the road.

As a side note, relationships last longer when each person has more physical space to live in, so think twice before cramming yourselves into that tiny apartment or single-wide trailer.

Honesty

Honesty is the brick and mortar in trust. There's a time and place to be honest, and that time and place is *most* of the time. The challenge is to be honest without hurting anyone's feelings. As a general rule, do not reveal things that are going to be unnecessarily destructive, critical, or nonproductive to the relationship. However, there will be moments when you will have to forego your own comfort, bite the bullet, and tell the brutal truth. This is a freeing experience, and any decent guy will follow suit and be honest, too.

Quality Time

There is nothing about technology that has freed up our time to do other things. Everyone is attached to cell phones, laptops, and PDAs. It's ridiculous. Shut off the phone and make a concerted effort to enjoy the peace and quiet of each other's company without interruption. Quality time alone is a must.

Pushing the Envelope: Return to Sender

I'm used to getting away with just about anything. I push the envelope, from the very beginning of my relationships, in an attempt to stretch the boundaries in case I need that freedom later on. One instance: A few years back I began dating Carly. I wasn't head over heels about her in the beginning, but I genuinely liked her. We ended up staying together for much longer than I had expected because she laid down the law and consistently made me adhere to it. I went from liking her to being fully committed to her. For example, I used to do something called "night splitting," where I would go out with some people earlier in the evening, and then meet up with other people later on. Carly didn't allow that. She said that if I wanted to see her, I would make plans with her for the entire evening. Otherwise, I could see her another time. I liked that, because it showed that she was stong, had convictions, and knew when to put her foot down.

Men like the structure of solid rules when those rules are reasonable and well timed. (Remember, be consistent on rules and boundaries, spontaneous on entertainment and fun.) The only reason Carly and I broke up was because she was looking to get married and, well, Bad Boys don't walk the plank that easily. Otherwise, she changed me!

A Word on Communication Foundations

When it comes to who calls whom, rather than following whatever guidelines your friends give you, it's best to make a declaration from the very beginning of the relationship that you don't follow conventional rules, and that he can call or not call whenever he feels like it, and you'll do the same. Getting rid of calling rules is one of the most liberating things I've introduced into my dating. Women love it because it removes a number of questions. No one likes waiting for the phone to ring. Most of us like a little anticipation, but there's a point where you, as a woman, should be able to say, "Screw it. I'm calling him to see what he's up to." Having said that, if you are ever in a situation where you don't know whether or not to "make the call," then it's completely justifiable to ask yourself two questions: (1) Why am I calling? and (2) Am I feeling confident enough to call at this very moment? If you are calling for the simple reason that you want to and you can deal with the fact he may not respond the way you might like, then go for it. The other thing to keep in mind is the age-old expression "Better to remain silent and be thought a fool than to open your mouth and remove all doubt." I have no idea who coined that phrase, but it makes sense. (You may recall that on page 151, I talk about laying down the law in terms of texting versus calling—you'll have to use your best judgment as to what kind of rules are best for your situation.)

Planting Seeds

I'm not talking petunias. In the very beginning of a relationship, guys will plant seeds in a woman's mind "just in case." These are what I call the "I told you so" seeds. They're mostly lame attempts at making sure they feel vindicated should they decide to move on.

The standard seeds:

• I just got out of a bad relationship and don't want anything serious.

• I'm so confused right now.

• I'm too young to settle down.

• I really have to focus on my job, so I don't have time for anything too serious. (*Note:* If a guy uses this one, ask him to explain how Clinton found time to fool around with Monica.)

These are the basic excuses—look for a wide array of variations on these themes.

However, if you happen to be with a "pro," you may hear something more like these:

• I'm looking for someone who understands me.

• I didn't have a great childhood, so I have trouble getting attached.

• You're just going to love me and leave me (reverse psychology alert!).

• I get bored so easily with life.

Pay attention, because these seeds are planted to kill two birds with one stone: Depending how adept he is at the delivery, he can use them as early "I told you so" seeds that emerge through the surface during the breakup, but also during the relationship to get you to feel bad for him and try to fix him. (We know you women are suckers for a broken wing and like to try to change men.) The latter strategy buys us time and ensures that our hooks will be in long enough to get the sex we want and enjoy the honeymoon stage.

The time to kill these seeds is now, at the very beginning. Have an answer/solution for everything he throws at you. Call him on everything so that at least if he decides to leave you later, you can make him feel like shit and force him to be a man and face the heart he's broken. For example, if he says, "I really don't want a serious relationship right now," you say, "Define *serious,* because I want to make sure we're both clear on the definition. After all, some people think sex is serious." Or if he says, "I had a bad experience with my last girlfriend, so I'm gun-shy," you say, "I'm not your ex-girlfriend and you look nothing like my ex-boyfriend, so I think we're in good shape." It's about letting him know you didn't just fall off the turnip truck. If you notice a seed and can't think of a quick response on the spot, store it for later, bring up the conversation again, and deliver your response. Keep him accountable for his words and actions.

Female Seeds

Since every man has an exit strategy, you need one as well. It's sad that you have to think about breaking up right when you've met someone, but if he's not right for one reason or another, you need to have a plan to exit intact.

Plant these seeds in his brain:

• The most important thing to me is honesty and trust. If a guy can't be honest, he's not much of a man. (Say it like you would never consider him in this group of men, as if you were speaking about all other guys.)

• It takes a while to get to know me. Men and women are different like that. The more you know me, the better it gets [wink is optional].

• I'll never ask anyone to give more than I'm willing to give, which is why I'm so generous.

• I killed the last guy I went out with with an ice pick because he broke up with me. [Giggle] Kidding.

The key here is to be very subtle but very clear: Think of it as sticking Post-it notes on his body for things he needs to remember if he wants you to be his girl. Should you catch him not following your "Post-its," simply remind him that he was at the meeting, and he'd better shape up. For example:

• You catch him in a lie: "People who lie are chicken; real men are brave."

• He's not opening up and getting to know you: Have your period last for weeks—if you get my hint.

• He's asking you to go out of your way for him, which he hasn't been doing for you: "Sorry, I have to fold laundry. Can't do that right now."

• He's being an ass: "Do you have a life insurance policy?"

Chapter 46

Below the Belt

I can't believe I'm going to tell you this. But I promised that this book would open the male dating mind for you, and if there's one thing men don't like, it's their own vulnerabilities. In this chapter I show you how to find your man's insecurities and use them for your own good.

I regularly hear women complain about manly-man boyfriends who could stand to be cut down to size every now and then. How can this be done? With the ultimate power move: by using the top four male weaknesses—hair, penis size, career, and height—to keep a man's ego in line. Any man worth his salt will take this technique in stride, remaining confident enough not to fold while you pick up some relationship power. Women who do this cleverly always come out on top.

Let me be forthright and admit that this is extremely high-level game-playing. But I've got news for you: The dating world isn't always fun. Sometimes it gets ugly, and you have to be willing to throw some mud here and there. My job is not to be nice. My job is to give you the skills you need to win and stay in control. With a perfect match, most of these things won't need to happen, but every situation calls for a different degree of toughness. I think it's better that I tell you the options, and that you apply them when you think they're necessary. Remember, you're dating men, not kittens.

Note: If you plan to use this technique as a means to have the upper hand in the relationship, then you need to use it sparingly, subtly, and wisely. Using this strategy carelessly can leave you with an angry man or no man at all, neither of which is pleasant. And you'll look mean. In many ways, men are more sensitive than women, and they are definitely more reactionary, which is why the success of this technique depends on the delivery.

Why Point Out a Man's Weaknesses?

Why on earth would you want to highlight a guy's vulnerabilities? You wouldn't want him to do it to you, right? The answer, though clichéd, is simple: All is fair in love and war. Every now and then, a woman needs a little help diluting that testosterone, and subtle put-downs might just be the answer. Many men have a bit too much ego for their own good and, frankly, they'll respond to an attack on their vulnerabilities in a way they won't respond to normal conversation. A subtle put-down is also a good way to get a man to slow down and pay attention to you, by letting him know that you see his deepest weakness(es). Men do it to you all the time, and now you'll know how to return the favor.

We Do It to You

Even though we may not comment directly, many men see a woman's weaknesses and use them to gain the upper hand in a relationship. Because women tend to be a little more emotional than men are, they often wear their feelings on their sleeves, giving men free access to information that can be used to manipulate them. For example, if we overhear you talking to a girlfriend on the phone about the size of your feet, we may use that to tease you. Or if you have a mustache, or constantly wear a sweater wrapped around your waist to hide your bum, we'll tease you about those, too. But by paying attention, you can use the same strategy he uses on you to take stock of his fallibility and let him know you're aware of it. He won't be so cocky and will tread a bit lighter once he knows you can see his intimate secret(s).

The Four Male Weaknesses

The top four male weaknesses are hair, penis size, career, and height, not always in that order. At least one of these weaknesses, if not two, is present in most men. It's up to you to find which one, and then gently let him know you're aware of it. Let's go through the list one at a time.

Hair

Men are sensitive about their hair if it's turning gray, falling out, or looking feminine. To a man, losing hair is tantamount to their losing prowess, sex appeal, or youth. A man is acutely aware of the fact that very few men look good bald, and he's scared that he won't be one of the elite. If he's smart, he'll shave his head when his hair starts thinning, and use that biker look to his advantage. If not, he's an open target. The same principle holds true if he's going gray early.

How to Break Him with His Hair

Once you've figured out his hair flaw, and after you've gotten to know him a bit, simply mention something like "It's no big deal when men go bald/gray, as long as they look good, don't you think?" Or, if you're commenting on a bad haircut, say something along the lines of "Nothing is worse than a bad haircut on a man. I saw this guy with the dorkiest haircut today." If this bait doesn't prompt a response, say, "Your hair is okay, but next time you get it cut, let me go with you." Take him down a few pegs by highlighting his poor choice of salons.

Alternatively, if he's bald or thinning, ask him what it was like for him to lose his hair. The tone of this entire interaction needs to be "It's okay, I understand," almost as if you feel bad for him, but that you're not superficial, so his appearance really doesn't matter. You could say something like "A lot of guys look good with shaved heads or bald. I guess it has everything to do with the shape of the head. You look pretty good." What you have just communicated is "Look, I know this is a weakness of yours, and if you mess with me, I'm going to bury you with this."

Penis Size

Since the earliest signs of puberty, we guys have been comparing ourselves with other men. The boys who got pubic hair first were more "guy." As men get older, we compare our penises with those of every man we see in the locker room (although we would rather die than get caught glancing), and of course, we weigh in on the Internet, looking at the lucky men of porn. Moreover, at some point in their lives most men measure themselves with a cloth tape measure (cloth because the metal can be cold and sharp).

My point is that the penis is a constant point of concern for us. I call it the GPS, global penis system, because our equipment truly does direct and rule our lives. Men will always make "small dick" jokes as a way to put one another down. Even if a guy is of average size, or slightly above, he can be made to feel inadequate.

Note: This said, if a man has an exceptionally small penis, it's best not to talk about it at all until you are long into the relationship and have built a loving trust.

How to Comment on His Primary Concern

When it comes to the penis, more is more. However, when it comes to commenting on the penis, less is more. The way to get that penis point across—without hurting him so deeply that he heads for the hills—is simply to call it by a name that connotes something little and cute: Brussels Sprout, Pickle, Twinkie. We hate that, and it gets us wondering how we measure up to your past boyfriends—not a topic we like to fathom. This quickly makes us just insecure enough that you can have the upper hand and lead us around a bit (not forever, so plan accordingly). How long this strategy works depends on how often you bring it up. The more often you mention it, the more we'll grow immune. As a rule of thumb, you'll get a few weeks of mileage out of it.

Another clever way to make a penis joke is to act like a guy, and do just that: make a joke you've heard one guy say to another guy. I could give you a long list here, but why not go and ask your male friends? They'll know a ton, and you'll have fun laughing.

If a guy is well endowed, then the way you can criticize him is by calling it a deformity. Try these on him:

- "Put down that club and fight like a man."
- "Well, if you ever run out of job options, you can always join the circus with that thing."

Career

Money is an aphrodisiac for much of the female population. Some women follow money as a career, trying to date anybody with a big checkbook. But even for women who aren't gold diggers, it's simple math to guys: No money, no girls. No sexy job title, no girls.

A friend once told me that men spend half their lives trying to become successful, and the other half trying to prove that their success wasn't a fluke. Men really need you to know that they are truly smart and powerful, not just lucky. Regardless of how rich or successful your guy is, he will compare himself with someone who is making more money or is more powerful.

How to Get Him Where He Lives

What to do? It's simple: Listen carefully to find out whom he puts down or talks about incessantly, and find one redeeming quality about that person. Then simply mention that quality in an off-the-cuff way. As in "Wow, Howard really looked great tonight, don't you think? That tailored suit was really becoming." Your man may jump down your throat when he hears it, but now you know you've hit a nerve. *When a guy shows anger, it's a weakness. His weakness equals your power.*

Again, if you want to gain a measure of control but make your relationship last, you need to make your comment in a way that indicates that you are okay with his job title and income. It will be abundantly clear that you are aware of money and status but are bearing with him. It's almost as if you are doing him a favor. Someone is always going to be richer and more powerful. He knows it, and now he knows that you know it.

Height

Height is something I've battled with my entire adult life, not because I'm particularly short, but because I chose to plant myself in an industry of giants. I modeled for many years, and was often the shortest person on the set. This was tough. After a while, it didn't matter so much because I was extremely successful in spite of my shortcomings. However, I never forgot it. My height always sat in the back of my mind as an insecurity. That's how I know that you can use height to put a guy in his place.

How to Cut Him Down to Size

Granted, if he's six-two, this isn't going to work. I guess you could make a statement like "It's more important how two people fit together than how they look side by side, don't you think?" Maybe that would get him thinking, but otherwise you have to use this ploy on those of average height or under—which, depending where you live, is around five foot nine and a half for men. For the tall boys, make them feel too big, and for the shorter guys, read on.

It's quite easy to make a shorter man's height a point of contention. Just look at him one day and ask, "How tall are you?" That will be enough. When he answers by questioning your question or giving you his measurements, compliment him on something unrelated. He'll get the point.

Plan B

Particularly confident men occasionally won't respond to the aforementioned strategies. So move to plan B, which is to create an insecurity where one previously didn't exist. It's best to pick a trait he's sure of yet not too confident about. Examples include his body, strength, intelligence, mechanical prowess, or bedroom abilities. Simply create a potential list of traits in your head, and then watch him to see where you can play with his mind a bit. Then slide in a subtle comment: insecurity is human nature, and even if he slightly doubts your observation, it will get him thinking and—*voilà*, he will second-guess himself. In his moment of second-guessing, you'll have just enough time to establish yourself as a worthy opponent and keep him on his toes.

Believe it or not, men like this challenge. We may complain and sound disgruntled, but your insults increase our interest in you, because we now have a goal: to prove to you that we are not weak, that our penis is fine, that we're not too short, and that we can afford to date you. And while we try to prove ourselves, you are suddenly in the driver's seat.

Keep in mind you should do this only with very strong men; the average guy will already be in "I need to prove myself" mode from the first day he sheepishly phones you. This strategy is ideal for the guy who is a good person deep down but who has just gotten too full of himself. Or you can use it on the asshole you're planning to dump anyway. Use as needed, applying a thin coat on the "good guy." Feel free to drown the "ass."

Good luck, and don't forget that the pendulum swings in both directions.

Chapter 47

Black Widows

For those of you who don't spend your hours watching nature shows, black widow spiders are deadly, poisonous arachnids known for killing and sometimes eating the male spider after mating. Nothing embodies the concept of a man-eating woman better than this little black creature. And guess what: they have a human form. Take a look at celebrity tabloids, and you'll see what I'm talking about—those cover girls who go from man to man, often taking them away from other women.

Now, I'm not suggesting that you subscribe to this behavior, or aspire to be a Black Widow. But these women are brilliant when it comes to dealing with men, and there is much to learn from them.

I've always been a Bad Boy, but I haven't always been great at dealing with women. I've lost many, many times and have made millions of mistakes. But, without a doubt, it was my Black Widow encounters that sharpened my relationship pencil to a fine point.

Who They Are

Black Widows are the female version of the Bad Boy. Somewhere along the line they developed a talent for leading men around like puppies. They're incredibly confident women who carry their sexuality on their sleeves, and they are Oscar winners when it comes to acting as if they couldn't care less if men called. They do not play by the same rules as most women, nor do they allow the watchful eyes of Mr. Prim and Mrs. Proper to determine how they'll behave. Because of this, they win more often than they lose.

When it comes to relationships, Black Widows don't even know the word *fair,* nor should they, because in the dating jungle, *fair* is not a winning philosophy. Do I like Black Widows? Absolutely. Do other men like Black Widows? Yes, they have no choice; the web these women weave is so intricate that by the time a guy knows he's caught, it's too late. She's already wrapped him up tightly and left him.

What You Can Learn from Them

For a Bad Boy, there is no greater challenge than going head to head with a Black Widow. Sparks will fly. It's like chess. We are on the same board, with the same rules, and only the strongest and cleverest will survive. You may think that this sounds crazy, but it's exhilarating. Here's what these women do that separates them from the pack:

1. They're unapologetically sexual.

2. They communicate as much with their eyes as they do with their bodies. They usually back up their gazes with a knowing smirk.

3. They have no problem blowing men off.

4. They know how men think, and manipulate every angle of our psyche. It's second nature to them.

5. They dress in a way that leaves their victim helpless.

The combination of all five of these traits makes up their "web." Lets go through each trait point by point.

1. They're Unapologetically Sexual

Imagine if you could act as sexually as you wanted, and no one could do a damn thing about it. Now imagine getting hateful looks from other women, but remaining unflustered, and using their glares as encouraging proof that you are doing something right. This is the world of the Black Widow. She is who she is, and she's not sorry. She has *sexy* down to a science; it's rarely cheap or sleazy, and always effective. Most often, true Black Widows are classy in appearance and behavior, but show an overwhelming *umph* when it comes to their sexuality. It's subtle, and not every woman can pull it off, but when they do, the male casualties amass.

2. They Communicate with Their Eyes

A Black Widow's eye contact is forceful and deliberate. Her eyes remain fixed on her prey, and seldom wander off. As well they shouldn't; she's sizing him up. It's as if she has a huge bullhorn and is screaming, "Look at me! I'm going to ruin you! I can see what makes you tick! *Please,* honey, you're already dead." With a slight smirk and a steady gaze, the games have begun.

3. They Blow Men Off

I've discovered that a wide variety of women have no trouble blowing men off to quickly end a fling or relationship, though Black Widows do it with a cold finality that can only be compared to surgery. They simply remove you without anesthesia. Not only do they blow you off with cold precision, but they make all their moves with confidence and accuracy.

4. They Know How Men Think

Just as Bad Boys have mostly female friends, Black Widows have mostly male friends. Their male affiliations give them insight, a pool of possible suitors, and the upper hand. Know thine enemy.

5. They Dress to Kill

Every piece of a Black Widow's wardrobe is chosen and worn in a way that leaves men helpless. Black Widows put their outfits together knowing full well their effect on the male species. Is it contrived? No. It's second nature to them. The point is they use their clothing to lure men with the accuracy of a surgeon and combine that accuracy with wits to snare their victim. The rest is history. If he's smart he'll survive; if not he'll be "eaten alive."

Q&A

Q: How do I act like a Black Widow without coming across as a bitch?

A: Black Widows are sexy, not mean. But they often get labeled as bitches anyway, because most men are sore losers who try to minimize their loss by calling Black Widows names. However, if you compliment a man on something genuine and let him walk away with a small amount of ego, you may avoid the aforementioned label. Although who cares what people call you?

Why You Should Befriend Them

If you need an example of how to dress, walk, and talk to attract men, then make friends with a Black Widow (good luck). Actually, Black Widows can make great female friends; they just seldom befriend women because other women have trouble dealing with all the attention they get. If I were you, I would suck up my ego and become friends with one of these man killers, to steal some of her secrets. Watch and learn.

The important thing to remember is that Black Widows are no different from Bad Boys. You don't need to become a Black Widow, or date a Bad Boy. Instead, just wrap your mind around how they think, and steal some of their tricks until your own dating life becomes easier. The best of the worst can help you feel in control of your dating life, and make you prosper.

How to Weave Your Web

Along the road, I've encountered some very clever Black Widows. Some I was able to outplay; others conquered me. Of course, the interesting tales are of the women who beat me at my own game. Here are three stories of Black Widows who made a mockery of me. Read and learn from my mistakes and from the skills of the women who beat me cold.

I Talk Too Much

It was an average night for me, sitting between two beautiful girls at an after-party in a nightclub a decade ago. I had no idea how difficult either woman would be to seduce. At that point in my life, I didn't have experience with every type of Black Widow, so I never saw this one coming. I decided that I liked the girl to my left, and began planting the seeds. Blah, blah, blah—I went on and on about this and that, becoming more entangled in her web, when all of a sudden, she turned to me, looked me in the eye without blinking, and said, "You talk too much." She paused a brief moment to see if I had a response, and then, seeing that I was stumped, excused herself to go to the bathroom.

My heart raced. What was I going to do? I do talk too much, it's true, so maybe I should apologize. No, apologizing is weak, especially to a Black Widow. And I was sure, by this point, that I had just gotten bitten by one. Okay, Steve, think. Back-paddling will get you up a creek, and apologizing will leave you vulnerable, but you have to take a chance on one!

As she walked back toward me, in what seemed like action-movie slow motion, I braced myself for impact. She wasn't looking at me, so I called her to come over. When she was directly in front of me, I looked her in the eye and said, "You know, you don't have to be bitchy. There's no need to be rude to me. You can be nice and I'll still like you. Give me your number, and we'll get together." To this, she stood back, took stock, and went off to find a pen to write down her number.

A few days later, I phoned her and arranged to meet her at a restaurant. I knew I had to show zero sign that I liked her, which wasn't going to be easy because not only did I consider her hot, but she was a major challenge—she had won the first round—and I was up for battle. As I've said before, if there's anything a Bad Boy likes, it's a challenge. I shut off my "Oh my God, I want you so badly" button. It worked. I sat down, ate dinner, and conversed with her as if we were two friends. At the end of the meal, I was walking her back to her apartment, and she invited me up (only because I had shown no sign of inviting myself up). Once upstairs, I opted to sit in the chair across from her rather than on the couch beside her. You could cut the tension with a knife, but I wasn't folding. I was going to play this out as long as possible. Then I made my move. I got up and put on my jacket to leave. A major risk, because she could actually have let me go.

She said, "Where are you going?"

"Home."

"Well, just tuck me in."

"Here we go," I thought to myself. Now she's playing hardball. She stripped down to her T-shirt and undies and hopped into her bed. I kept my jacket on, pulled the covers up around her, and kissed her on the forehead. Needless to say, she broke. She pulled me in and began kissing me. I walked home that night with an ear-to-ear smile. I had won. I had beaten a formidable Black Widow.

But au contraire. She got what she wanted and then blew *me* off. When I tried for my "buy one, get one free," she laughed and asked if my roommate was interested. (My roommate was a woman!) Checkmate. She won. I lost.

Lesson learned: Sticking to a a long-term plan, staying calm, and leading a man into your web will lead to success with your more challenging dates.

Don't Hate Me Because I'm Beautiful

One of the greatest powers a Black Widow can exercise is the power of manipulating the effect her body has on men. One strategy is to flaunt it and then tell you that she's sick of guys being attracted to her only for her physical attributes. Confusion ensues. She's playing a victim of her bootylicious self, pretending to be a girl she's not, a woman with a great figure who has no idea how to handle men and, therefore, keeps getting used. Nothing could have been further from the truth with Katrina, but I bought it hook, line, and sinker.

I couldn't even breathe the first time I saw her. A woman's body can do that to a man. We were introduced by a mutual female friend. I chose to keep my mouth shut, conserve my oxygen, and arrange a meeting. We had dinner, and she came back to my house. So far, so good. We kissed, rolled around with our clothes mostly on, and then she left.

"Hey, she likes me," I thought. Not so much. The next day I phoned her to tell her how hot she was, and upon hearing so, she became disgruntled that I had focused on her body instead of her personality.

I switched my game plan to cater to her need to appeal as a "serious woman." What a mistake! She had just won, and I didn't even know it. She was testing me, and I had failed. She did this by creating an environment where I would have to prove that I wasn't superficial if I wanted to sleep with her, which effectively put the ball in her court and kept it there. I fell for it and went down the road of "getting to know" her and acting like I wanted to be her boyfriend. What an idiot I was. The "I wanna be your boyfriend" routine bored her because so many men had tried it before. I should've dealt with the obvious: she had a hot body, I wanted it, and too bad if she didn't like that fact. Hell, she wasn't going to look like that forever. But it was too late. We saw each other a few more times, things ended messily, and I moved on.

What I want you to see here is the power that Katrina wielded by using her body as a point of contention. Men are fixated on a woman's body, so anything she says regarding this matter is going to be taken seriously. Take this example, and water it down to fit your own situation. You'll get amazing results.

Lesson learned: you should often go with the obvious. Katrina was aware of how hot her body was, and she used it accordingly. I should have seen that and not fallen victim. Same goes for you: if you notice that a guy has a gorgeous body or a sparkling personality, then chances are that's the exact thing he'll use to try to pull you under his spell.

Heart on Your Sleeve

If I had to name the most common mistake that everyone makes in dating, it would be too obviously showing someone that you like him or her. This is an error I've made a lot. When you fall head over heels for someone, it's difficult to hold back your feelings, but you must. And, on numerous occasions, I haven't. When I met Andrina, I was blown away. But the more I liked her, the farther she ran. When I met Kylie, she liked me only when I didn't show interest. When I started chasing Natasha, I may as well have been chasing my own tail. I could go on and on, but I won't waste your time. If you want to know how to combat the I-like-you-too-much affliction, don't worry, we'll get there in the next chapter.

Lesson learned: Some women like to hunt as much as guys, and I should never have denied them that luxury. Nor should you deny men that luxury. Engage men in a way that makes them hunt you, and feel free to employ some of the time-tested tactics of the Black Widow. Remember this: no relationship is a waste. You are just learning how to play the game. Bad Boys get beaten all the time, and sometimes the eight legs of a Black Widow are better than two trapped behind fishnets. Think about it.

Chapter 48

Auction Annie

I want to tell you a fable about two ladies I like to call Annie and Edna. That is, Auction Annie and Ebay Edna, as I call them. They're best friends and great dating advisors.

Auction Annie, with her long gray ponytail and yellow sundresses, would spend many hot summer days on her front porch talking with Edna, a beautiful seventy-year-old woman with big brown eyes and smooth, soft skin. They would sit and chat for hours about their beliefs about men. I'd wander by, sit on the bottom step, and listen to them debate. Annie, perched on the glider alongside Edna, would slowly rock back and forth—she had to rock slowly or Edna would complain she was getting seasick. They told me they liked me because I was everything that was wrong and everything that was right about men. "Here comes the devil," they would say as I approached.

On one particular afternoon, I listened to Annie explain that once you've found a great man, you had to make sure you didn't cling to him like dryer lint. Annie would always say that the "first thing people do when they meet someone they like is put all their eggs in one basket. They never leave a little breathing room." She went on to explain that it raises the stakes too high when you jump in head first. If things fail, you're doomed. Annie took a long sip of her ginger ale as Edna said, "Annie, tell Steve what girls should do."

Auction Annie's Top Four

1. Think of dating as an auction: Each man has a price tag. Some are worth it, some aren't. Try to distinguish who's who as soon as possible and don't get "attached" to a guy who may seem great but isn't worth the aggravation or the price you'll have to pay for being with him.

2. Once you meet a guy you like more than all the others, "go through the motions" of continuing to date other men. This may seem silly, but you have to have a distraction. Being distracted keeps you from being "too available," because being too available robs your new object of desire of his most primitive instincts: to hunt.

3. Compare Prince Charming with the other guys you are going out with and take stock of all their most redeeming qualities.

4. When you've already found someone you like, you are much more at ease while on other dates and can, therefore, think more clearly about yourself and what you truly want from a man. Ladies should use that time to see the "forest through the trees." Meaning: you won't feel that you have to make it work with this one guy and you won't be so immersed in infatuation that you miss his true colors—colors that could be both good and bad. Being on dates with other men creates the psychology that you have options, which in turn creates clarity.

I asked Annie why a woman had to date other guys if she'd already met someone she liked. Was it necessary? Without stopping the glider, Annie leaned back, drew in a deep breath, and said, "Boy, I wish it weren't that way, but I can't go and reinvent the wheel. That's just the way it is. If people had more willpower, they could make a new relationship work without the need for distractions. But how many people do you know with enough willpower to resist a new love?"

Edna's voice, a comforting blend of southern drawl and stern authority, suddenly blurted out, "The best part of doing what Annie says is that no relationship is a waste of time. You're always learning something and having fun."

Annie looked over at me and said, "You'd better listen to her."

Edna continued: "It takes a while before you truly get to know everything about someone: what they're like when they're hungry, what they're like when they're traveling, what they're like when they're happy or sad. You may not like everything, but at least you're making the best of it and having fun along the way."

She told me that she had so many girlfriends who would pine away for just one guy and overlook all the others. Girls get together with a man and begin to think he's the only fish in the sea, and before you knew it, they were trying to *make* it work instead of *letting* it work. Granted, all good relationships are work, but you shouldn't ever feel like you're kidding yourself into settling. "Your love should go to the highest bidder: the guy who loves you and understands you the most," Edna said.

Ebay Edna's Love Recipe

1. No relationship is a waste of time.
2. Have fun with the guy even if he's "not the one."
3. Pine is for furniture, not for men.
4. Don't push too hard; let things unfold naturally.
5. Don't sell yourself short.

Edna admitted that there was nothing wrong with being utterly single sometimes, but she insisted that men were wonderful and that even if he wasn't "the one," you could still go out and have fun with a guy. "Women settle because they get lazy or they fall more in love with the *idea* of the relationship than they do with the man himself," Edna explained. "The best thing a woman can do is to make sure she's a great catch and then look around for just the right fisherman."

Then both Annie and Edna looked at me and asked, "What are you going to do? Are you ever going to get married?"

"I don't know. Maybe. But I'm not having kids, that's for sure," I said. "In the meantime, I'm going to have a lot of fun."

"I bet you are." They both laughed. "The devil always does."

I smiled, got up, stretched, kissed them both on the cheek, and began following a cute ass in a pair of jeans down the sidewalk.

Q&A

Q: I just met a guy whom I really like and I don't want to date anyone else, but you say to date more than one person. Why should I?

A: I'm not suggesting that you get intimate with other people. I'm suggesting that you keep your options open, and remember that the playing field can change drastically in a week. You also will come off as a better, nondesperate catch to your man if you're busy and you legitimately have other options.

Part V

Mating

Sometimes it's hard to figure out how your relationship is going. You know that you've made it past the third-date barrier, yet you can't quite figure out what he's thinking. Will you be together for the next three days or the next thirty years? Well, ladies, I'm here to help you figure out what's really going on so that you can get the upper hand in a relationship. I'll break this discussion down for you by relationship stage: "Early in the Game," "End Game," or "Game On!" This section applies to all men, but gauge how you use the information by the type of guy you're with, as well as where you are in your relationship.

Chapter 49

Stop in the Name of Love

Your gut instincts will tell you what's going on at every stage of a relationship, and I want you to get used to trusting those instincts and acting on them. Don't second-guess yourself. After you've been dating awhile, your gut instinct is what will tell you whether he's on his way to full-fledged boyfriendhood. As an intuitive woman, you'll notice subtle changes in his demeanor that will clue you in. And your mind will say, "Hey, I think he's changing."

Take a look at these gems for signs that he's really trying to make it to the next level with you.

1. He leaves you alone in his house or apartment and possibly even gives you a key. This is a telltale sign that he's committed, because all men know women like to snoop. What he's saying is: I trust you to not go through my sock drawer; all you'll find is socks. (You, meanwhile, need not to mess up and snoop! All men have something to hide, be it pictures of ex-girlfriends or "keepsakes." These women are out of his life, but he may hang on to photos or clothing for sentimental reasons—nothing you need to worry about right now.)

2. He makes room in his medicine chest for your toothbrush and all those girly things you use to beautify the hell out of your skin. This means that though he may not be ready for the two of you to live together, he's not ruling out the idea, and he likes feeling that you're part of his life.

3. He calls you just to say he's thinking about you—even if he doesn't say, "I was thinking about you." Making a random phone call in which he doesn't have any pressing news to tell you means he can't stop thinking about you. Don't force it out of him. Let him be cute, and just know that if he did call, it was because you were on his mind.

4. He can fall asleep holding you. Most people like to fall asleep on "their" side of the bed. But when I'm falling for a girl, I can hold her until she falls asleep, or until my arm is all pins and needles—whichever happens first. I've even woken up in the morning with my arm around her.

5. He leaves his cell phone unattended, knowing you won't try to check his address book, text messages, or incoming/outgoing call lists—and that if you did, he would be completely safe. This is a big one nowadays.

6. He mentions something he wants to do with you in the future, such as a restaurant he'd like to try or an activity for the two of you next season, such as a future ski trip.

7. He introduces you as his girlfriend.

8. He shows small signs of jealousy or is protective when other guys are mentioned.

9. He buys you little things even when it's not a special occasion.

10. He discovers the mysterious world of "foreplay." A guy who is really starting to like you will begin making that extra effort in the bedroom. Ready for this? He may even start asking you to be specific as to what you like and don't like, so that he can please you.

The beauty of these changes is that he notices them, too. He suddenly realizes you've "affected" him, and he's not the same way he was with other women. This makes him both happy and scared: happy because he knows he's made a good choice in you, and scared because he wonders if this is the "real deal." But he'll keep moving forward, however cautiously, and you'll know that you did all the right things to make him feel good about himself, and good about being with you.

Chapter 50

Making This Dog a Woman's Best Friend

always tell people that the day-to-day dynamics of a couple are what keeps them together or pulls them apart. Some people refer to this concept as "putting the cap back on the toothpaste." You both gotta do it.

If you break down twenty-four hours in any relationship, most of that time is spent out of bed, doing normal activities. Think of all the things you do together every week: shopping, running errands, exercising, doing chores, and dealing with each other's work stress. All of these tasks create a thousand little moments of reality. Can you help him? Can he help you? Can you be a shoulder for each other to cry on? Can you and he support each other's moodiness and self-doubt? These are the true tests of a bond, and are what create the solid foundation on which successful relationships are built.

That means that you have to get along and be able to talk to each other, and become each other's best friend. That may sound fairly rudimentary, but you'd be surprised at how many women (and men) don't take full advantage of this downtime. And when I say "downtime," I mean the hours that aren't spent staring into each other's eyes and kissing. You have to prepare yourself for the end of the honeymoon without losing the romance. And it truly is a very fine balance between being your man's hot paramour and being the person he hangs out with the most—his best friend.

You see, guys are more likely to cheat on a girl if they feel she's "just a girlfriend," but they won't cheat on their best friend. Good men are very loyal to their friends, and are also more likely to go out of their way to help them.

You make him your best friend by understanding him, by seeing his side of things, and by getting him to talk about his skeletons. You don't need to completely empty his closet, but if you can hand-pick a few things he might consider embarrassing and let him know you accept him for his flaws, he'll love you and feel safe. (You have to be genuinely nonjudgmental here, or it won't work.)

But as you know, there's always risk, and here there's no exception: You don't want to fall into the "friend" category completely. You don't want to become his sister, or one of the guys. When I use the term *best friend*, I mean someone he can feel comfortable being vulnerable in front of. I don't mean *friend* as in "We're just friends." That would change the relationship and hurt those oh-so-precious moments of passion and romance.

How do you perform this balancing act? By always acting like the sexy girlfriend. By making damn well sure he never forgets the reason you two first hooked up: you're one hot momma, but one whom he can trust with his secrets.

It's a very important balance to strike and will take some trial and error to achieve. Here's an example of a situation where a girl was my best friend yet also never let me forget how sexy she was.

In my line of work (entertainment), there are extreme highs and extreme lows. One day I feel like a rising star, and the next, like a loser. On this particular day, I came home and told my girlfriend that I had lost a great job. I explained that the producers had chosen someone younger. For the most part, I was inconsolable. She sat quietly and listened. When I was finished whining about how messed up my business is, she gave me the hard facts about the cold realities of my chosen profession. She reminded me that no one had forced me to choose this field, that it wasn't always going to be fair, and that if I couldn't handle the heat, I should get out of the kitchen.

I liked that she wasn't babying me. Then she encouraged me by reminding me of my past successes, and by saying that part of the game was just hanging in there. Once I was securely "off the ledge," she grabbed me and kissed me and told me all the ways in which I made her feel wonderful. She was essentially complimenting me in ways that made me feel masculine.

Most men don't want to seem weak, fallible, or vulnerable in front of women. But if you can find a way to support them in their struggles without showing pity, then you'll solidify your best-friend status. (Meanness or siding with the opposition is out of the question—this is not the time to subtly put him down for one of the four weaknesses!) To keep the sexy role intact, all you have to do is seal your loving support with a kiss—or anything else sexy—and help us get our mojo back.

What This Means for You

1. Don't baby him.
2. Listen to him.
3. Give him a little dose of tough love.
4. Seal every support session with a kiss.

Above all, you're his sexy girlfriend, the one *he wants to spend time with*—not his nag, not his sister, not his therapist. Sexy, friendly, fun.

Chapter 51

Surrender

Relationships require seduction. If you seduce a guy, he will be a good boyfriend. End of chapter. Good luck. Let me know how it goes.

I'm kidding.

You know how a man spends months in the thralls of courting you, attempting to win your love? Well, you, too, must seduce him into being your man—and into choosing you as his only girl. The easiest way to do this is simple: by rewarding him when he is considerate and shows that he respects you. This means that when he buys you dinner, helps you with your cleaning, swings by the grocery store for you, or carries your piano up four flights of stairs, you should reward him with praise and kindness. You're subtly telling him what makes you happy, just as you would with a puppy: When he does something right, you toss him a treat. The psychologists call it "positive reinforcement." I call it "winning your man."

When I first started dating Carrie, I thought that at best we would be a one-month fling. (See Chapter 33 for a discusion of the dating clock.) But Carrie did something the other girls didn't: She went out of her way to tell me and show me how much she appreciated my gestures. She was affectionate, and she returned the favor whenever she could. The more I gave, the more she gave, and before I knew it, we were both invested in the relationship.

My friend Arianne tells me that this might seem obvious. "Steve, women might think of this as 'setting the tone' of a relationship," she says. "When a gal does something really nice for her man, he'll probably do something equally nice for her next week. And if he doesn't, she should leave 'im!"

Well, Arianne, I wish it were that obvious, but many people behave with a sense of "entitlement," and don't show their appreciation nearly enough. Showing your man some appreciation is like throwing him a bone. You're rewarding him for being good, showing him that being a good man has its benefits. If you set that standard for your long-term relationship, you're good to go!

Back to Carrie and me. I liked when Carrie would tell her friends about something I had done for her. She did this in a matter-of-fact kind of way, with a hint of bragging. Men like to be bragged about. We like that you are proud to have us in your life and that you see us as masculine and generous. Carrie would also cook me dinner from time to time, and once she showed up with a new CD she'd heard me mention. It was a sexy CD, and she benefited from that gesture as much as I did; we both heard the music on that one.

Carrie had a unique way of making me feel masculine and needed—which is exactly how I wanted to feel. She never had to worry about my treating her poorly, because she and I both knew (wink-wink, smirk-smirk) that she was just fulfilling her duties in the relationship by helping me be chivalrous. Just as it was my job to open doors and pick up the dinner tab, she understood that there were certain social behaviors *she* needed to engage in to build the harmony in the relationship.

Relationship roles are hard for some men to figure out these days. It's a different time now: Women are equal, if not better, than men in many areas of the workforce. (I worked as a model for many years, which is a job where women make more money than men for the same task.) Women are adept at juggling jobs and kids, single moms are everywhere, and you're all capable of being independent. You don't need us for basic survival anymore, and we know it. Frankly, we don't think you need us for much of anything.

But we want to be *needed,* not just "wanted." So what to do? Do we stick to the old-fashioned values of paying for things and lifting heavy objects, all for the reward of being "lucky enough" to be in your company? Nah, that ain't gonna cut it when we could just hang out with the guys instead. What will cut it is finding creative ways to show us that you don't see the relationship as a one-way street. Ladies, you have to step up to the plate and *show* us that you need us. Show us that you appreciate us, thereby seducing us into wanting to do more for you. It's cyclical. You be a good girlfriend; we'll be better boyfriends.

How to Be a Great Girlfriend

I'm sure you've been in a relationship where you did all the giving. It sucks. You probably felt that you were being used, and were running up an incredible emotional debt. That's how men often feel, and we don't like it any more than you do.

I'm sure that you're kindhearted and keenly appreciative of your guy, but you can't just think it. You have to *show* it. Here's how:

1. Learn how to give a massage. Most guys don't make regular visits to the spa, so a good massage every now and again goes a long way.

2. Cook something. Anything. Just cook. When a woman cooks for me and it comes out charred, I'm thrilled. Don't forget, boys will chow down on cold pizza and a beer at 9:00 a.m. My point? The bar is set so low that you have no excuse for not cooking occasionally!

3. Make the bed when you stay over. I never make my bed, so when I hop out of the shower and see the bed made, I smile from ear to ear . . . it's so girly and so great.

4. Ask if you can add a feminine touch to his house or apartment. As long as it's not a wall-size poster of kittens playing with yarn, you should be safe.

5. Sit us down, look us in the eye, and say thank you. List several specific things we've done for you and tell us how much you appreciated them.

6. Help us organize something: our bills, our house, our desk, anything. Most of the guys I know could use some sort of help in this department. Make sure your help is wanted, then go to town.

This chapter may not seem to teach *seduction* in the common use of the word, but it's the little things that bring us closer, and the closer we are, the more we want you. And how do most men show you how much they want you? Ah, I knew you'd get it.

Chapter 52
Spank

Contrary to what this chapter title implies, there's nothing kinky about setting rules and making sure that your partner abides by them. There is no way around it. You must create rules whether you're having a fling, are dating, or are in love.

In Chapter 45 we talked about laying the groundwork in the very early stages of dating, starting each new relationship on solid ground regardless of where it might head. In this section, we move forward to talk about how to establish long-term rules of engagement, the kind of things you need to take care of once you and your man have been together for a while—say, six months to a year—and are ready to take things to the next level. It's about picking and choosing the rules you'll need to keep in place if you're destined to have a long relationship.

These rules will be your guidelines, your gatekeepers, and the brains behind your heart. You can't trust your heart. If it were up to your heart, you would take in every stray animal you saw. Your love life is no place for an animal shelter! Feel with your heart, and act smartly with your brain by setting up guidelines to turn to when your heart tells you to act like a moron or sell yourself short.

If you're single right now, write down a list of reasonable rules that will make you feel happy and respected. As soon as you meet a new guy, refer to the list. I don't have to tell you not to let him know you've done this; he'll think you're crazy. But when your heart is involved, I repeat, you can't always trust your own judgment. I'm sure you can't count the many times you've let guys get away with behavior you shouldn't have stood for. For this reason, it's good to have a net to fall back on when you're walking the love tightrope. Each of you will have her own rules, but here's a list of things that are general no-nos.

Your Man's No-Nos

- name-calling;

- showing up late;

- cheating or dating other girls if it's understood the two of you are monogamous;

- inappropriate PDA (public displays of affection)—i.e., using hands for anything other than hugs or a soft pat on the bum;

- lying;

- canceling plans within four hours of when you are supposed to go out, unless there is a genuine, unforeseen, emergency;

- poor manners;

- forgetting to call (the "I didn't have time" excuse is not okay if he said he would; he should call to say, "I'll call you later"); and

- being rude.

You want to be careful to set up rules that you can also adhere to, thereby setting a good example. I can't tell you how many girls have double standards, and it's horrendously unattractive. I can hear you now: "But Steve! In Chapter thirty-seven you talked about making cutesy little rules you can break, such as 'No feet on the table.' What's the difference?" Well, ladies, the difference is that here we're talking about the standards that you will live by for the duration of your relationship. If the relationship ends, you want to leave it feeling that you didn't sell yourself short. Also, your guy will be able to tell the difference between goofy rules and serious standards.

By implementing basic rules from the get-go, you'll avoid the doormat syndrome in which you let a guy get away with too much. Stick to your guns!

By now you know that I'm Mr. Analogy, so here's another one for you: You go to a yard sale and see a ceramic lawn elf that, for some strange reason, you just have to have. In your mind, you decide that you'll pay twenty-five dollars for it. That's your rule. But when you ask about the price, you're alarmed that the crotchety neighbor sitting in a lawn chair smoking a cigarette through a hole in her throat wants fifty bucks for it. The negotiation begins.

"Can you do any better on the price?" you ask.

"[Coughs] Give me thirty-five bucks for it."

Inside you're thinking about how badly you want this. "How about twenty?"

"Nope. Sorry." Long cough through her tracheotomy hole. "It's thirty-five."

Now is the moment of reckoning. Do you walk, or do you pay too much and experience buyer's remorse an hour later? You decide to walk. You give that miserable Yankee an eye roll and head to your car.

You have to maintain the same mentality in a relationship: be willing to walk if the deal is no good. If you think it's hard walking away now, imagine how difficult it will be to walk away once you feel months or years of emotional debt come creeping into your head. People spend their *entire lives* in bad marriages for this reason. If your rules/standards are in jeopardy, walk away!

When and How to Set the Rules

The time to set up the rules is in the honeymoon stage of the relationship, as soon as you know it's going past the four- to six-month mark. You can do this in two ways:

1. By literally (but nicely) telling him what you will and will not put up with, particularly on points that you perceive might be future problems. (Ladies, you all know if your man is a player!)

2. By calling him on grievances as soon as he steps over the line.

Either way, be clear, concise, and to the point. Don't let there be any room for bargaining or backpedaling. Be friendly if it's a first offense, but be stern.

Why is this so much easier said than done? Because you can see the prize. It's so close. You want him so badly. You just know, with a little more time, he'll break down and follow your rules and start treating you with the respect you deserve. Wrong. He won't. He's a dog who's gotten used to jumping on the bed and peeing on the carpet, and there's no going back.

Don't worry—your rules won't make him leave you. If he leaves, he would've left anyway, and this way, it happened with you in control of the situation, standing up for yourself and making sure that you got treated well. Stand your ground.

I've made huge mistakes with women: I've believed they would eventually change if I could just overlook the fact that they were being rude, behaving poorly, or not abiding by my baseline standards for a good relationship. Don't make the same mistakes yourself. Even in love, certain rules apply. And sometimes those rules require that you walk away from the deal. If you aren't willing to walk, then you're selling yourself to the lowest bidder, and we don't want that.

Don't Abuse the Rules

Women can get away with murder in this area because although we guys have our own standards, we will overlook them if we haven't gotten you into bed. Our visceral urge for sex is so strong that some of us—especially Bad Boys—will let you put us through hell while we bide our time to get you naked. Don't abuse this power, ladies. We'll end up resenting you, and when we finally do get what we want, we'll look for the first chance to put you in your place. That often comes in the form of dumping you.

Should one of us break the rules, don't automatically break up with us. We're human beings with flaws, and sometimes we make mistakes. Learn the difference between a loser and a guy who's slipped. Get to the bottom of the problem and see if you can fix it. We're in this "disposable" society, it seems, but people should never be disposable. Save *disposable* for the razors you shave your legs with—and please stop using mine. (You think I don't notice? I can totally tell!)

Chapter 53

Put Up Your Dukes

In the beginning of a relationship, many women will walk on eggshells while attempting to avoid the first fight. Guys know this and will sometimes see what they can get away with before you blow your top. Don't let him push you around. This is the time to step up to the plate and hit him out of the park. If he's got any balls, he'll stand up to you and maturely work out the problem. If he doesn't, you've killed two birds with one stone—you just found out that your man of the hour has no backbone, *and* you stood up for yourself. Home team wins!

I have a confession: sometimes I enjoy fighting. I do it because I'm bored, to try to get a woman to open up, or to see how clever she is. Fighting about benign topics is a form of entertainment for me. Whatever your reason, when you get in a fight, remember that the fight isn't a big deal. What's important is how you resolve it. A good resolution can bring you closer as a couple or build unhealthy walls. One of you has to be the mature one and keep the discussion mature and productive. If it has to be you, just do it. Another point to keep in mind: don't head off on tangents. This is not the time to bring up sins he committed in the past. Stick to the point, listen, and don't point fingers. But be direct, brutally direct, with men on all topics, with the exception of anything approaching the male ego. Fight away, but not at the expense of his ego. Attacking it won't do any good anyway, because he'll go into defensive mode.

In conclusion, it's good to fight sometimes, just fight fair and be mature about it!

Chapter 54

Hold On Loosely

No matter how old you are, go online and look up the lyrics to the song "Hold On Loosely," by the band 38 Special. I can't cut and paste them here; the publisher of my book would send me a bill you wouldn't believe.

I know, you're still on dial-up and need me to explain all of this, so let me tell you about my ex-girlfriend Sarah. Sarah was amazing. So smart. So chilled out. So great. I met her in a health food store. Why was I in a health food store? Because I'm a healthy male, with an appetite for women who look great in ponytails, jeans, and T-shirts that read SAVE THE WHALES. I walked up to her as she was browsing the tea section.

"Does tea really have more caffeine than coffee?" I asked.

She looked over at me, calmly picked a box from the shelf, read it, and handed it to me. "This one doesn't." She went back to browsing.

She was ignoring me—smart move on her part. Needless to say, she saw that I wasn't interested in the caffeine content of Sunshine Splendor Tea, and decided to flirt with me when I kept the conversation going.

We ended up going out, and when we got closer, I began my normal Bad Boy antics. A man's first impulse is to think that all women are out to "trap" him. I kept our time short and sweet, and employed other strategies that would keep her from getting "too attached." But she let my lame excuses roll off her back. She didn't fight me when I left her after midnight to go sleep at my house.

Instead, she gave me that overtly disapproving girlfriend look, making it silently clear that she disapproved, and then let me leave without making an issue of it. That was strange. Why didn't she make a big deal about it? Did she not care about me? Did she have someone on the side?

She was, without spelling it out, sending me the following message: *I could leave at any time.* She liked me, and it would have been nice if I had stayed over, but if I didn't want a relationship, she would happily let the door hit me where the good Lord split me.

Always free to go? What a concept. Herein lies the concept of *hold on loosely.* Guys are afraid to commit, and we don't like drama, right? Well, when it's clear that a monogamous, committed relationship has developed, things work best when the woman gives the man enough slack to hang himself, all while holding on loosely until he feels safe.

> Note: This chapter doesn't apply to guys who are coming over for a little action. A man needs to show that he's in a relationship with you, demonstrating concrete actions over time, before this strategy will work.

In Sarah's case, I didn't hang myself. I wanted to be with her because I knew that the door was unlocked and that I could leave. She gave me nothing to resist and nothing to fight. I was free *and* in a relationship. I was just as free to *stay* as I was to *go.* Is that possible? It was for Sarah and me.

Let me explain. Before Sarah, I had been in several relationships that became too demanding too fast. I could feel that my girlfriends were bothered by my reluctance to quickly play house. But guys need some breathing room to get used to being committed. For many men, *committed* is a four-letter word.

How to Reel Him into Your Clutches

You almost need to trick your man into thinking that more together time is what he wants. It's not a game. It's a little reverse psychology. For example, make it clear that you do want him but only when he values the importance of sleeping over and giving you a little bedtime story as the two of you doze off.

One way to do this is by making him think the sleepover is more a matter of common sense than an attempt to play house. Let him think he's just crashing there instead of doing the walk/drive of shame for no reason. If you're dating a tough guy, lay down the law on a night he's chilled out. Tell him, "No, tonight you are staying here. Now get in your PJs. I'll meet you in the bed."

Second, make him comfortable. Treat him like a guest for the first few slumber parties. Make it fun.

Third, get up before he does, make coffee, and ask if he has time for breakfast. Then tell him that you have some stuff to do, so that you can kick his ass out after breakfast.

You will eventually win! Slowly but surely, he'll see your house as much more inviting than crashing in his weeks-old SpongeBob sheets. He'll actually look forward to the luxury of a sweet-smelling, clean-sheeted girl's bed. Once he's settled in, your place can quickly become his favorite hotel.

Sarah had a special personality that allowed her to be genuinely chilled out in this department, but I don't want you to fake who you are. All I ask is that you take a breath and see whether there is some free rope from which to cut him a line—with ample slack. Every couple's dynamic is unique, but anyone can exercise "hold on loosely" to fit her needs.

Chapter 55

Why We Don't Want to Cuddle at Bedtime

Your man is happy. He's in your bed, you've finished romping, and he's now ready for sleep, building a cocoon of pillows and blankets on his side of the bed. All is well with the world. Then your words pierce the silence.

"Honey, will you spoon me?"

Uh-oh. His face drops.

When this request comes up, he will most likely begin by trying to dodge it, instead offering an obligatory back pat. Surely a back pat will suffice.

"Honey, that's not spooning."

He'll then grudgingly comply, leaving his cocoon to move into full cuddling position, sensing the big smile on your face. While you're calmly drifting off, he'll roll his eyes, hoping that you fall asleep quickly so that he can get back to his side of the bed and get some rest.

Why are men like this? There are a few explanations:

1. The most obvious is that **spooning and cuddling are not comfortable sleeping positions.** Unless a couple's bodies happen to fit perfectly, spooning and cuddling can be all elbows and tossing and turning. Most single people are used to sleeping alone, and the only thing they hug is the extra pillow. Pillows don't have bones.

2. It takes time to get used to another person's body and sleeping habits. In the beginning, co-sleeping can be very uncomfortable. If you insist on being held too early in the relationship, chances are he won't get a good night's sleep, won't want to stay over that often, and will wake up a Cranky Franky.

3. Cuddling is not considered very masculine by men. Have you ever heard the boys picking on a sad buddy? They laugh and squeak in a high voice, "Hold me!" Some of us guys see cuddling as the equivalent of needing a blanky or a stuffed animal to feel safe. We'll get over this complex in time and see it for what it really is: intimate and relaxing. But we have to ease ourselves into it and know that *the guys will never find out.* Breaking that last rule means that all bets are off!

How to Break Him into Cuddling

If you like being held by your man, it's best to start slowly. Begin with an "extended hug" before you fall asleep. I love it when a woman gives me a long hug, a sweet kiss on the neck, and then goes to her side of the bed. I also feel that it's a good compromise to have some part of your bodies touching as you drift off. Good options include two feet touching or gently holding hands. Over time, the long hug and body touching will extend into the night.

Warning Signs

Cuddling—or a lack thereof—can let you know your man's feelings for you. Don't read into any hesitance early in a relationship; some men just move slowly. However, if he never seems to touch you in a nonsexual, lovey-dovey way after a few months, you need to address the issue during daylight hours. Ask him why he rarely touches you, and listen to his answer. Give him the benefit of the doubt, but make sure it's not a warning sign that he's not crazy about you. Once you have clearly explained to him that it would mean a lot if he held you for a few minutes, he needs to comply.

I went out with a girl who was a cold fish come sleep time. At first I thought it was because she was really tired all the time and didn't want to be bothered. A couple of months in, I realized that there was no excuse: she was just selfish.

You may have noticed that this "he/she is just tired" excuse comes up a lot. Anytime you tell yourself that your man's not doing something because he's tired, busy, or stressed, try asking yourself whether you're making excuses for him. Chances are he's not stepping up to the plate, and you're letting him get away with it! Fatigue/stress/busyness are one- to five-day excuses. Not month- or year-long ones. Better to realize it now than later.

As time passes, and as the two of you get closer, you should be looking for affection to increase. If it doesn't, take the warning to heart.

Sometimes a lack of nighttime affection can also indicate intimacy problems, tipping you off to the rest of the "iceberg" lurking below. Now would be a good time to head to warmer waters. You'll know what to do. Trust your instincts on this one, and drop him if you need to.

Finding the Happy Medium

There's a lighter side to cuddling, and taking advantage of it will help you get even more cuddling. I once lived with a girl who loved the "leg over," her maneuver for draping her leg across both of mine. Early on, I forbade the leg over. "No leg over," I would whisper. She ignored me, heavily sprawling a leg across my knees. I inevitably would try to push her leg gently off me, and we would end up laughing and wrestling. We made a game out of it. Each night, I pretended that I didn't notice that she was making her move, or I strategically placed my body in the leg-over-prevention position— on my back, both knees up. She'd always find a way around it, draping her leg across my face. I'm laughing even as I write this.

My point is that you need to find your man's happy medium. Figure out his most comfortable sleeping position and watch where his body naturally falls in those first few minutes when he closes his eyes and begins to drift off. (These are precious minutes that, if disturbed, set your man up for a night of tossing and turning. They are not a time for discussion.)

In general, let cuddling evolve along with the relationship. Until then, give it a rest.

Chapter 56

Smooch

K issing is incredible when it's with the right person *and* that person knows how to kiss. After all, the eyes may be the window to a person's soul, but the lips are the front door. Do you know how to kiss? Have you practiced? Would you consider yourself a great kisser? Here's a primer in how to make sublime kissing last for years.

What Kissing Reveals

Kissing exposes a lot about a person. It's similar to watching a man dance: in a minute or less, you get a clear picture of his personality while he's cutting the rug. Kissing is no different, telling you who that person is and how he feels about you in a few brief moments.

When a man and a woman touch lips for the first time, it's either magic, mediocre, or mayhem. I personally prefer awful to "Eh?" At least with awful, you want to try it again to see if it was just a bad night. With "Eh?" you know that it's probably as good as it will get, and it's time to look below the lips . . . to the hips.

I can tell what type of woman I'm with from the very first kiss. That one kiss can be surprisingly influential. Our potential as a couple is on the line. If she runs her fingers through my hair and gently pulls it while kissing me, then she's passionate. If she has tight lips, places her hands in one place on my back, and is awkward, then she's uptight. If she gently grabs my face and holds on while kissing, she's nurturing. If she balances her kissing with little breaks of soft conversation, she's a very confident woman. And, finally, if she is all over the place and slobbering on me like a Saint Bernard, then she's a little bit too much. Meaning: She'll most likely be overbearing or is making up for some shortcoming by being overzealous. Disregard the latter if she's drunk.

Obviously, our potential as a couple will also depend on other factors—what sort of relationship we're both looking for, where we are in our lives, etc. But kisses, in their own way, communicate a lot of that information. I will say that I've been on dates with a girl I wasn't initially crazy about, yet when she kissed me, I was so blown away that I wanted to know more about her. The opposite has held true as well: I've really liked a girl, yet when we finally kissed, I was let down and looked for a way out.

What kind of information can *you* gather from the way a man kisses you? Everything, if you're paying attention. But *please do not overthink a kiss!* Maybe on the fifth kiss you can take a moment to analyze, but in the meantime, just let it happen and listen to your gut. These are the things you should look for post fifth kiss:

1. If he kisses you long and often, he wants to really get to know you.

2. If he kisses you all over your face, he adores you.

3. If he kisses your bum, literally, he is totally crazy about you.

4. If he runs his hands through your hair while he's kissing you, he knows what most women like (note to self).

5. If he starts fumbling, trying to disrobe you, as soon as you start kissing, he needs to simmer down.

6. If he kisses you only before sex, you need to keep an eye on that. He's showing signs that he's not genuinely interested in you.

7. If he kisses you and doesn't break eye contact, he could be falling in love, or he's really trying to seduce you. Sometimes these two are hard to distinguish.

How to Kiss

Good kissing wins your partner huge bonus points, and is not a skill that you'll soon forget! A *great* kisser is truly rare. I've kissed my fair share of girls, but I can count the great kissers on one hand.

Kissing properly is all about going slowly at first, learning each other's face and mouth. Does he have a big nose or a small nose? Does he kiss from the right or the left? How does he feel about tongue? It sounds silly to break it down like this, but when I kiss for the first time, I'm looking for a synchronized connection—a spark. Aren't we all?

First, the hygiene issues:

- Make sure your lips aren't too wet or too dry.

- Personally, I don't like the taste of lipstick. Hint, hint.

- Fresh breath is a must. If you've both just left the same restaurant, maybe there can be an exception. But bad breath can seriously ruin a moment. BreathRx did a study and found that 61 percent of men and 91 percent of women said a romantic situation was ruined because of bad breath. Invest in fresh breath; it's worth it.

There are exceptions to every rule, but in general, when it comes to the kiss, try a little of everything. Although there's no need to chip a tooth in the first week of a relationship.

Instead of going in with old habits and preconceived notions, pay attention to how he reacts. Those reactions will tell you exactly what he likes, giving you all the information you need to proceed. When you are kissing a man for the very first time, play with these things:

- Kiss just his top or his bottom lip softly.

- Don't just kiss his mouth. Kiss his cheek, his neck, and his forehead.

- Don't go hog wild with your tongue on the first few kisses. Be conservative.

- If you've got small lips, it's best to kiss a bit softer. If you have big lips, try not to swallow us whole.

- Close your eyes and forget all these kissing advice tidbits and just kiss. Let yourself go and really enjoy it. Get completely lost in the moment. Who gives a damn how you're doing it? Just *let go!*

How to Make It Last

In my mind, kissing is one of the most old-fashioned, wonderful activities that a couple can do, and it should stretch over a lifetime. In other words, there is no expiration date on kissing. Making out is a blast that should last.

Once you've had some great make-out sessions with your partner, it's time to set up some stealth relationship guidelines so that kissing extends beyond the honeymoon stage.

First, let me explain what kissing means to men. Kissing is a form of foreplay. It's that simple. We kiss because it's a way to get you and, subsequently, ourselves heated up. We kiss because we are trying to get somewhere; in most cases, kissing is a means to an end. Yes, we like to kiss, but this is also one of the few dating areas where men can successfully multitask, and we take full advantage of that. We can be kissing and undoing a bra, or kissing and rubbing your bum. We can kiss and watch the TV behind you. We kiss as long as we are doing other things as well.

I sometimes crudely refer to kissing as "waiting on line to get on the roller coaster." Kissing can get like that. It can become a chore for guys. Most of the guys I know love making out with their girl, but it's because *she* set it up that way, by laying the groundwork. She enjoys kissing, and now she reaps the rewards. In the past, I've been really bad about not kissing enough, which is how I know it's a problem. Once men are in full swing and are having "bed time" on a regular basis, we figure, "Why wait in line? Why not just get on the ride?" It's pathetic, but true. We like other things more than kissing, and our GPS (global penis system) is always guiding us in that direction.

What's a girl to do? For starters, she can teach us that making out is fun, and that it doesn't always have to lead to sex. Sometimes you can just make out with us and then stop. That's your prerogative. That's right: making out *just* to make out. What a novel concept!

Be careful not to get too hot and heavy. To do this, keep the kissing innocent. You don't want to appear to be a tease. We don't like that. But if you make out with us and then go your merry way, we'll find it fun and unpredictable. It will get us excited. You'd be amazed at how long you can sit and talk and play kissing games if you make it fun. You'll hear me repeat this a lot: Men are just big kids. Make anything fun, and we'll play.

Again, it's very important that you start this early on so that you train us into the kissing habit. XOXO.

Kissing Goodbye

Kissing also provides a direct window into your partner's feelings for you. Sadly, as his feelings of romance begin to disappear, so does the kissing. The absence of kissing can be a big fat warning sign that something is up. I personally think the lack of kissing is bad; I don't like it one bit. First, it stops during dates, next in the bedroom, and before you know it, kissing has been reduced to the kinds of pecks on the lips you'd give a friend. When that happens, reevaluate your relationship and figure out where the problems lie. Start keeping your eye on the exit.

Chapter 57

Effective Affection

Now it's time for me to dish out strategies for increasing your cuddle time and PDAs. I want you to get your hugs and hand-holding without resorting to violence. Yes, ladies, we men have felt you gently beat us with pillows in the name of affection, whining, "Come *on*! Cuddle me!" There is a better way. Let me help you.

Not receiving the affection you need is no fun. And, unfortunately, a lot of people are more willing to hug a stray dog than a person. Adding insult to injury, sometimes you have to *ask* for affection. Why should you have to ask for something that should come naturally? I admit it: I've had to *ask* for a hug before, and I've even had to *ask* to hold hands. It's ridiculous.

But I'm an eternal optimist, and there ain't no mountain high enough.

The Get-Your-Affection Plan

In Private

Men are always compared to dogs. Well, ladies, now it's your turn. Have you ever watched a dog take his nose and shove it under your hand to be petted? The dog's owner catches on immediately. Launch a similar strategy yourself. Next time you're watching a movie or sitting on the couch, take his arm and put it around you, sinking the back of your head into his chest. On every greeting and departure give him a big hug. He'll get the hint and start initiating on his own. Any decent man will realize that you like affection, and if he wants to keep you, he'll put out.

In Public

The way to go about getting the public strokes you need requires you to be patient, and to hold back a bit on your own PDA distribution. Begin by resisting your urge to throw yourself in his arms while you stroll along the river. By simply walking next to him, you're showing him your strength and independence. You're telling him that you don't need reassurance.

Next time you're crossing the street together, reach down and clasp his hand. I know that you still need hugs, but the PDA needs to grow in equal measures with the growth of the relationship.

Get things moving in the right direction by creating your own Kodak moments, stopping him in random places and giving him a small peck and a naughty grin. Move to the next level (a passionate kiss) when you are coming home at night. Men feel safer giving PDAs if they don't think that the whole world is watching. Eventually he'll realize no one cares, and if they do, chances are they're envious. We all want that movie moment where the person we're with can't resist embracing us and kissing us deeply.

Warning Signs

If the man you're with is having trouble in either the public or private affection department and you've followed my tips, you may be witnessing the first signs that you're dating someone you shouldn't be with. Granted, some people are reserved and don't believe in PDAs, but if your man is rarely affectionate, and you've been a patient partner and addressed the issue directly with no response, then get rid of him. There can be many reasons for his resistance, none of which is good: Some guys fear being affectionate in public because they don't want anyone to see them. Who is "anyone"? Is it an ex-girlfriend he has "unresolved" feelings for? Is he dating other women? Or is he just a cold fish with intimacy problems? These are not problems you should have to overcome.

I'll admit that it's difficult to analyze your love life when you're in the middle of it. I'm a relationship expert, and it's tough for me, too. But what I've seen work is careful reflection in moments of solitary space. Don't be paranoid, but look at what is *really* happening. Look at the actions and events more than the words and the promises. Remember that PDA is not an acronym for "pretty damn aggravating."

Chapter 58

The L-Word Jump

Have you ever gone skydiving, or jumped off a high rock into a lake? You know the sick feeling you get in your stomach just before jumping? Opening up, letting go, and jumping into a relationship can bring on a similar feeling of nausea. That nausea is the body's reaction to fear of injury. Think about that. No one wants to get hurt.

Once a relationship gets to a certain "height," someone has to jump. One of you has to take the risk and tell the other person what you *hope* you both are thinking—that you like each other. There have been smiles, hugs, and longing looks, but now one of you has to step up to the plate and put the cards on the table. But how do you decide when and where to make the kind of bold statements that could leave you open to rejection?

There are a couple of problems with jumping:

1. If your partner sees that you've opened up, and are expressing feelings he doesn't share, he may feel pressure to lie and not hurt your feelings. You'll assume that he feels the same way, which could cause you to move forward in the relationship, only to realize later that you were misled.

2. He may say nothing at all, neither denying nor accepting your overtures. This can leave you extremely confused, and scrambling for any hint that he feels *something*.

No matter what happens, the future is never certain when you finally jump. There will be that moment of "free fall," where the comfort of the landing is uncertain, but that uncertainty is what we should all embrace. It's how we know we're alive—by taking calculated risks and letting go.

Why You Need to Tell Him

If the feelings seem to be there, they need to be articulated. Articulation is good because once both parties' feelings are out on the table, you can build on them or decide that, maybe, you've made a mistake and need to change paths.

Early in the game, you need to do this to confirm that you are not making up the relationship in your head. We're all quirky people who like to see the optimistic side of things. Letting your feelings out is your own way of saying, "I'm not insane. You like me as much as I like you, right?"

More important, both men and women have a way of deluding *themselves*, and *each other*. We pretend that things are different from how they really are, and we sometimes blindly stay put. But in a conversation about honest feelings, the words have nowhere to go but in our faces. Sometimes it takes a good in-your-face conversation to wake you up. If your boyfriend can't deal with the reality of how you feel about him, then you'll find out. The sooner you know how he truly feels, the better.

How to Tell Him

Whatever your worries might be, it's important to take your jump with an attitude that you're doing it for *yourself*. You're not doing it with expectations of returned love. This is a time when the expression "Life is short" comes into play. What are you waiting for? You believe in love and in telling someone how you feel. If he doesn't feel the same way you do, who cares?

You don't have to get gushy and dramatic when you reveal your feelings, and you don't have to drown your boyfriend in one sitting. My advice is to take little leaps. Tell him a little and see how he responds.

Examples:

- "I really like you."
- "You know I'm crazy about you."
- "I'm really glad we met."
- "I have so much fun with you."

If he responds well, tell him a little more. For example, you could list several things about him that you enjoy and describe how you haven't found these things in other people. By being specific, he'll trust you really mean it, and find you endearing. This is not easy, because part of you will want to follow the philosophy you see in all those romantic comedies (rush in and tell him he's everything to you) or, worse, listen to your heart—and not your head—and let the cat out of the bag way too early and with too much intensity.

You have to balance seizing the day with acting intelligently. A good way to do this is not to let all your feelings and emotions well up inside you until you're ready to burst. If, all of a sudden, you let loose a cascade of your amorous feelings toward your loved one, he may be overwhelmed by the "emotional tsunami" and not be able to swim through it.

When you reach a point where you need concrete confirmation that you're both on the same page emotionally, then sit his ass down and tell him how you feel. Make it simple, nonchalant, and to the point. Cross your fingers and hope that he says he feels the same way.

Truth is, you'll most likely never feel completely safe to let go and jump, but jump you must. So be brave, look before you leap (keep your eyes open and be aware of whether jumping is a good idea or not), and then do it.

What-If Scenarios

There are always weird "I told him, and then he said . . ." scenarios. Let me clear some of them up for you.

1. He likes you more than you like him.

Tell him you like him, too, but that it takes you a long time to open up. Say that you've been hurt before and this is why it takes a while. But also tell him you're glad he's opened up. You need to encourage this behavior in case you need it down the road! Do not patronize him or say he's sweet; that's like nails on the chalkboard (or in the spleen) to us.

2. You like him more than he likes you.

If you spill the beans and he replies with a "Thanks, that's nice," there will be a moment of awkward silence and then you'll say this: "I like to tell someone how I feel when I feel it because sometimes I feel it one day and then don't the next, so I think it's best to get it out." Then act like his response hasn't affected you, and go throw up somewhere where he won't hear you.

3. He ignores it and doesn't seem to pay attention.

Make him pay attention (use your imagination) and make sure the TV is off and he's not preoccupied. Say, "Listen, dumb-ass, I'm trying to tell you how much I like being with you, and if you ignore me, this conversation will take on a whole new flavor. Got it?" Then smile sweetly.

4. You tell him how you feel, and he tells you he doesn't like you.

Tell him that you opened up and said those things because you were suspicious he didn't feel the same way, and you wanted to get it out of him so you could decide what you wanted to do. Tell him that it's your way of getting "closure." Then repeat the private vomiting from scenario 2.

5. A male friend tells you he likes you, and you don't feel the same.

This happens all the time. It can sometimes take the form of passive stalking, i.e., a guy who pretends he's your friend but is really enamored with you. The easiest and best thing to say is "I like you, you're amazing, and you're my friend, which is why I won't lie to you. I don't like you like that and I'm not going to fake it. It wouldn't be fair to you or me. I can't just pretend. You wouldn't if it were the other way around. [Guys like logic.] I wish I did feel like that, because you're great!" The idea is, the more ego he leaves with, the faster he moves on and leaves you alone. Tell him sooner rather than later—as soon as you're sure yourself. Though your instinct may be to avoid the confrontation, ignore that instinct.

6. He tells you, and you don't believe him.

An occupational hazard of being a Bad Boy is that sometimes we fall for a woman and she doesn't take us seriously. Every now and then, a Bad Boy really does like you, and is not just keeping you around until he gets bored.

I've been in this position before, but it always turns out that I'm treated like the boy who cried wolf. And you know what, that's just tough luck for me. Some women have experienced my kinds of tricks and won't be fooled again. Even when I truly like them (or even love them), they don't trust me. I don't blame them. If I like you enough and you've been a good, honest woman, then I'll spend the extra time to build trust. In your case, you can think of that extra time as working with a net. If he bails, it won't be so sudden, and you'll feel less bamboozled.

7. You're talking to a Bad Boy.

This advice will work on most men, but particularly Bad Boys. In general, I would recommend that you never tell a Bad Boy (or any noncommittal type) how you feel unless you are confronting him because he has hurt your feelings or is obviously misleading you. You should give him as little to work with as possible. Translation: he may use your emotional vulnerability to manipulate you.

Most of the Bad Boys I know, or the men with a heavy dose of that streak in them, will be vague about how they feel for *as long as possible,* so as to not be pinned down. They do this because it's not *really* lying (but it ain't telling the truth), and it leaves them the option to move in or out of the relationship depending on their whims.

Well, that may be *their* strategy but, tough shit, it's not your strategy, nor is it your job to wait until they come around. If you start to feel that the relationship has been meandering, then it's time to be a little more specific with what you expect from the man based on the quantity and quality of the time you've put in. Be ruthless, be specific, and commit. Don't do this by giving a long speech that begins with "Where is this relationship going?" Instead, tell him that you really like him, and then start being less available. Make it clear through your lack of availability that if he wants to be your man, he's got to get his shit together.

Chapter 59

Love Is a
Four-Letter Word

How and when do you tell a man you love him without scaring him away?

Counterintuitive though it may seem, those three little words, if uttered at the wrong time, can push him away. It doesn't make sense, but it's true. That simple phrase "I love you" can strike fear in a man if he hears it at the wrong moment.

That fear is actually a good thing. The fact that when he hears the L word, it causes a reaction in him, indicates that he takes love and commitment seriously enough. You know that he has morals and a heart.

Then, of course, there's the other side of fear, which is . . . fear of commitment and intimacy. That side of fear is lame. We must all go forward bravely.

> Note: Going through life making decisions based solely on fear of the outcome is not truly living! You can tell him I said so.

This said, do not go forward with alcohol. People who have been drinking always blurt out, "I love you, man," whether they mean it or not. Stick to sobriety on this one.

How to Drop the L Word

Saying those three little words feels good. And if it feels good, you should do it. However, there is a time, a place, and a way to ease a person into the idea that you love him. Spread these steps out over at least a week, if not longer:

Step 1

Begin by telling your guy that he's very "loveable." This isn't saying *you* love him; it's saying that he has potential and that you *could* love him.

Step 2

Next say, "You know, I really care about you."

Step 3

Say, "I really like you." Make sure that both of you are comfortable saying these things back and forth before you move to step 4.

Step 4

Now it's time to sit his ass down, look him in the eye, and ask him how he feels. You'll have much more power if you ask him to speak first. (Need I remind you of the advantage of the person who waits a split second when playing rock-paper-scissors?) Listen to how he stumbles around, and pay attention to his body language. This will help you guide your own words effectively.

Step 5

If you're still not quite sure where he stands, let him know that you are falling in love with him, and that you know there is a difference between *loving someone* and *being in love.* You're looking for the *in love.*

Does it seem pathetic to have to perform a five-step process just to tell someone you love him? Yes, it is pathetic. However, timing is everything. Think of love like a present. Like any gift, there are certain ways to wrap it and deliver it for maximum enjoyment. Let's imagine that you've bought me a new car. That's a great gift—but not if you run me over with it when you deliver it. Love is the same way. It's best to take it slowly and go through a process, making sure he can drive and that he knows how to work the car before you let him take the wheel.

Love is work and if either of you "quits" working, your love will die. So when someone tells you that he loves you, take it in and feel the warmth, and then put your feet back on the ground and keep working on the relationship. Men and women are the same on this point. Remember this.

"I Love You" or "I'm in Love with You"

As I've said, there's a difference between "I love you" and "I'm in love with you." Be very careful to get a concrete response that contains the words "I'm in love with you." If you say, "I'm in love with you," and he responds with "I love you, too," ask him what he means. Have him define *love* for you, and don't back down until he gives you a definitive answer.

Why all this microscopic inspection of the different levels of love? Because the truth is in the details, and the details can determine whether or not the two of you are on the same page. *In love* is something much more chemical, much more ethereal, and much more overwhelming and committal. A man can say he loves you and not see a romantic future with you. But if he tells you he's in love with you (and isn't lying), then he's committed and is looking to the future you'll spend together; he can't see an expiration date.

Warning: Lovers of Love

Depending on your age—the younger you are, the more often it happens—you may come across one of those men who pops "I love you" out of his mouth with aplomb. In his tiny head, he may even think that he does love you. But the truth is that his feelings are as temporary as the weather. He throws those words around like a Frisbee: I love pizza, I love my dog, I love the color green, and, oh yeah, I love you. He's careless and immature, a bull in your china shop. Be on guard for too-early utterances of the L word. Just because he says he loves you today doesn't mean that the feeling will remain in perpetuity. He may be fickle, he may be shallow, or he may be more in love with the idea of love. That's why you take it slow, giving yourself the luxury to build and discover along the way. Women are just as guilty of doing this . . . sadly, I know for a fact!

Saying Is Not Always Believing

My friend Kelly told me that sometimes women will tell a man they love him with the idea that, if they say it, eventually they will grow to be in love with him. I'm sure men do this as well. That's not only deceptive, but also extremely selfish and immature. Like a spoiled child, you're carelessly misleading someone into hanging around until you decide what you want to do. Don't do that. Because while you're deciding on love, your partner may be becoming more and more entwined. The day you decide, "Nah, I'm not going to fall in love. I'm dumping you," will be the day your partner is heartbroken.

Don't Freak Out

Some people fall in love faster than others. All that truly matters is that both outcomes are eventually equal—that you're both at the finish line together eventually. My point here is that it's not a race; people fall in love at different speeds. Is it necessary that you both have the exact same amount of love for each other at the exact same moment? No, it isn't. As long as the relationship is two-sided, the love will ebb and flow; it's normal. The question is, what to do if he is falling faster than you, or vice versa? It's never easy to wait, or to catch up. My suggestion is to do this:

• If he's falling faster than you, and you need to slow him down: Spend more time doing things together in mixed company, make sure you do a few things on your own each week (Sunday night is a girls' night), and if he's really falling too fast, start casually talking about an ugly divorce you just heard of where the wife killed the husband with a weed whacker. This should wake him up.

• If you're falling faster than he is and want him to catch up: Start to change things a bit. Begin to casually break habits the two of you have formed, including restaurants, bedtimes, and anything that you've done as a couple more than twice. Play a little hard to get again, and get very interested in his passions/hobbies in a nonannoying way.

Basically, what you are doing is changing the temperature in the relationship depending on what you want to be cookin'.

Bliss

You tell him how incredible he's made your life, he looks you deep in the eyes and says the same thing in his own words, and you both fall deeper in love. It's that simple, and that possible.

Chapter 60

Helter Skelter

There are a few foolproof ways to set off alarm bells in a man's head and unintentionally prod him into breaking up with you. Most women unknowingly employ these methods repeatedly, and then can't figure out why they're single. While your girlfriends may coddle you, I'm here to address your culpability and tell you how to stop scaring off men. The truth will set you free, so here's some straight talk.

If you want to scare him off, do any one of these things:

- ask if he wants children . . . in the first few weeks;
- ask where the relationship is going . . . within the first month;
- gain a lot of weight, dress slovenly, or don't take care of the feminine aspects of your body;
- become overbearing, moody, or difficult; or
- expect him to pay for everything.

These are the typical things that women do to send us running. I'm not saying that there aren't valid reasons behind these behaviors. Nor am I ignoring the fact that you may have been through a crisis that made you temporarily question your future and become overbearing. But a successful relationship is a two-way street, and you need to sit down and really understand your part in relationship failures—and how men interpret your behavior.

Dooming Behavior 1: Ask If He Wants Children

You have the right to know if you're wasting your time with a man who doesn't want a family. But I believe that the question you should be asking is, "Would you be a good father and husband?" And the only real answer to that question is to spend time with him. There are many aspects of a man that go into being a responsible father, and you will see those clearly over time. If you're not willing to spend the time to answer one of the most important questions you will ever ask, you're clearly not ready to have children.

Asking us too early or with a tone that makes us think you're "shopping" for a husband is a turnoff. We don't want to think you have a mental checklist that we have to abide by. And your leading questions are somewhat useless anyway, because a guy can tell you anything to appease you. Still wanna know? Talk *about* children instead of launching an interrogation. If babies are your dream, and the man sitting across from you has no interest, he will probably feel guilty enough to tell you so. And men who do want children will often bring it up in offhand conversation anyway.

Dooming Behavior 2: Ask Where the Relationship Is Going

I've mentioned that sometimes a guy can meet a girl, listen to what she says, and determine exactly how long the relationship (if you venture so far as to call it a "relationship") will last. This doesn't happen every time, and in fact it often applies only to women who fall into one clichéd category or another: for example, the needy girl, the husband shopper, or the let's-fool-around girl (yet another reason why consistent unpredictability is so great).

What I'm speaking of now is the relationship where the guy actually likes you. But he's still a guy, and commitment isn't something most of us men are born into or naturally inclined to engage in, and when you ask us, "Where is this relationship going?" we can sometimes feel backed into a corner. Therefore, let me answer, once and for all, for all men: *We don't know.* Really. We don't have crystal balls at home. All we know is that, so far, we like you. And, to us, the "liking" part is what makes it fun and exciting, not the "knowing where the relationship is going." And, ladies, in your corner of the ring, the mere asking of the question speaks volumes about your personal outlook on the relationship: if you have to ask that question at all, then there's a problem. When you ask us that question:

1. You appear insecure. This is a major turnoff.

2. You give the impression that things aren't going the way you want them to, which is also not flattering to us or to you.

3. We figure that no matter what we tell you, you'll believe us (e.g., "Oh honey, I see a bright future for the two of us"). Meaning: we think your desire to hear what you want to hear is greater than your desire to pay attention to reality and just go with the flow.

4. It sends the message that we may be on a female relationship time clock. "He has to be in love with me by *this date,* engaged by *this date,* planning the wedding by *this date,* and picking out the names of our four children no later than three years from now." (Say this in Charlie Brown's voice: UGH!!) It's amazing how one little question can have such a negative effect on men, but it does.

Dooming Behavior 3: Let Yourself Go

This next one is tough. Not all men are shallow. But when it comes to sex, we *are* visual. Remember that when we met you, we were *attracted* to you. If you looked a certain way, then we probably want you to remain that way, if not to improve. That's not to say we won't keep loving you as you age, but we don't expect dramatic changes such as your gaining twenty pounds or forgetting to wax. We may love you for the inside, but we want to have sex with the outside. Before you start harping about double standards, yes, this is a two-way street, and if your boyfriend gains significant weight, you're more than welcome to gently say something. I'm not saying you have to look like a skeleton. No man likes that. But it is important to stay relatively close in physical appearance, weight-wise, to how you were when the two of you met.

If you're still questioning my logic here, ask yourself: Does your partner want a friend or a lover? He already has friends. Lovers are built for lovin'. A cuddly bear is fine. A slob? Not so fine. Sex is an important element in a relationship, and both partners need to make sure that they continue to excite each other.

As an added incentive to put in a bit of effort, men automatically define *self-care* as *self-esteem*. And self-esteem is sexy.

Dooming Behavior 4: Be Overbearing, Moody, or Difficult

We love Glinda the Good Witch, but we won't put up with Lauren the Bitch. Growing up, we were forced to deal with the bad moods of our mothers and sisters, but we certainly don't have to deal with yours. Why would we listen to you rant when we could sit alone at home with a beer or watch the game with the guys? While of course men understand reasonable discussion and moodiness—we do it, too—we find prolonged difficult behavior to be annoying and time-consuming. And we Bad Boys have seen it so many times that we know what presses your buttons, and sometimes will even intentionally do so in the hope that you'll get sick of being difficult and chill out. But we'll probably leave first.

You will always get more bees with honey than with vinegar. If you're unhappy inside, please manage your issues and *then* start dating. Take it out on your therapist, not on us.

Dooming Behavior 5: Expect Him to Pay for Everything

Money matters. Gold diggers can disregard this section, as it doesn't apply to you—you have bigger problems. For the rest of you, good men want to take you out and make you feel special, but they also expect a little return on their investment. We're very cost-benefit oriented. This return can come in the form of home-cooked dinners once in a while, small gifts, and your paying for things. Just like you, we want to feel appreciated, and everyone, male or female, enjoys a loving freebie. Once in the relationship, you may find that going dutch or taking turns paying is the best solution. Money doesn't grow on trees, but ugly sticks do. And when you're cheap with us, it's as if you fell out of the ugly tree and hit every branch on the way down.

I leave you with some food for thought: Most relationship books spend endless chapters reaffirming the woman's role in a relationship. But sometimes you do and say stupid things that are the equivalent of shooting yourself in the foot. So take a moment to sit down and evaluate your past failed relationships. Don't beat yourself up, but take a good hard look and see where you might need to improve.

Uh-Oh

When a man decides he wants to break up with a woman, his goal is to have the least amount of resistance possible. We don't like to see women cry, we hate hearing you yell ("How *could* you?!"), and we despise drama. This all makes us feel guilty. Therefore, we avoid it at all costs.

We often achieve this by slowly easing out of a relationship, a process that could take us weeks or months. That's right. *We break up long before we break up.* We are mentally done with you far in advance. A bell goes off in our heads, and that's it: we're turned off. This can happen a month or more before we actually split. Women are often shocked when a brand-new ex finds a new girlfriend within days of ending the old relationship. But in most cases, he's been on his way out for months, scanning his options, and exiting when a new woman appears. It's that simple. We sometimes look at girls like stones in a river we're crossing; we don't hop to the next one until we're sure it's a safe leap. No one likes getting wet.

Lucky for you, our own slowness gives you ample time to get your wits about you and make your move. He'll be so busy preparing for "departure" that he'll never notice you've been taking notes. And he definitely won't expect that you've read this book, have paid attention to the early warning signs, and might beat him to the punch.

But how the hell do you know he's leaving? You always know. Frankly, you don't even need to hear it from me, because women have something that most men don't: intuition. You're good at reading people, and chances are you've seen a change in his behavior and expressed your concerns to your girlfriends repeatedly. Just listen to yourself talk on the phone.

The only problem? You second-guess yourself. Insecurity and human nature tell you it's your fault, and that you can change it. And you don't act on the signs. To make matters worse, we know you do this, and we use it to our advantage. We patiently watch as you go through stages of denial and self-doubt and arduously try to fix things. And we don't actually break up with you until we can comfortably say, "She's done. She's tired. Breaking up with her now will come as a relief." It's a victory for us, however melancholy. We can leave easily.

In case you have any doubt we're on our way out—hey, that rhymes—I'm going to list the warning signs so you'll have no one to blame if you don't take the beginnings of your partner's exit seriously.

• We slowly *start spending less time with you*. We're working late, going to games with the guys, and grabbing brews at the local hole-in-the-wall. Women frequently misread this stage as a growing form of comfort together, and see it as contentedly living separate lives. "Oh, he's just out with his buds." But you noticed, didn't you?

• We are *no longer romantic*. The dinners, the sex, and the sleep-overs drop off precipitously.

• The *passionate kissing turns into quick pecks*. Particularly note that there is very little kissing during sex.

• This is a tough one: in the event that we do have sex with you, we close our eyes and *fantasize about someone else*. Sex and love come from two different places in a man's brain, so if we're in the mood, we may do it anyway. You're not a mind reader, so just pay attention to *how you feel* during lovemaking. Chances are, you'll feel like he's removed.

- We try to get you used to *looking at us as a "friend."*

- We give you *the dreaded pat* during a hug—that should make your skin crawl.

- You catch us in *small lies.*

- We *start fooling around with someone else* and, in our minds, we justify it as okay because we figure we're done anyway.

- We *try to start fights* so that we can have an excuse to leave. This is a very low-level strategy and is used by impatient guys not skilled in the art of departure.

The upside? God gave you instincts to see these signs loud and clear. Trust them and act on them.

If He Does Say Goodbye

Very few women will calmly say, "You broke my heart. You really hurt me. You didn't have to lie to me." Very few women speak directly like this and let a guy know that they're on to him. By being calm, both in voice and gesture, you reach into his heart and pull it out. We expect you to be upset, but we don't expect you to be brutally honest in a very direct and human way. We'll feel that, and even if we don't show it, it will affect us. It's part of making a man culpable for his actions. Let him know you weren't just some joy ride. You're a woman. A person. Not a toy. For extra effect, say this with a note of pity.

Your Escape Hatch

Remember how we talked in Chapter 45 (under "Female Seeds") about hatching your own exit plan early on? Well, if things aren't going well, now is the time to pull the rip cord. Use the ultimatums you stated early on ("Honesty is the most important thing to me," "I'm not cool with lying," "You need to go out of your way for me from time to time") as your excuse for setting him free. You told him what he needed to do, and he didn't do it. Fair game!

Chapter 62

Mayday! Mayday!

Breaking up is no fun, whether you're the "dumper" or the "dumpee." But getting dumped is worse, and getting blindsided—unexpectedly dumped—is *the* worst. I don't want you to get blindsided. So we're going to take care of you, and teach you how to know when to leave.

In every relationship, the writing is always on the wall, and you need only read that writing and make a decision. It pains me to tell you how to be the "dumper," but I will. Why? Because I've been dumped by women whom I *didn't even like*, and it still hurts. Sometimes I deserved it and sometimes I didn't. But every time it happened, I *thought* she had had no idea what I was planning, and then *wham!* She beat me to it, while I sat there slack-jawed, stunned, before limping back to the locker room to rethink my game plan. I'll now show you how to use the element of surprise to get out while the getting out is good.

This chapter assumes that you have already identified serious problems in the relationship. For those of you who still need to do some soul searching, do not pass Go. Back up and read Chapter 61, "Uh-Oh."

SOS

Once the ship is going down, it's best to let it sink. Cut your losses. This does two things for you:

1. it saves your self-esteem; and
2. it may prompt him to scramble to try to keep you.

The result: the entire power dynamic of the relationship lurches toward you. That feels great. Much better than being blindsided. And that's how you should have felt throughout the relationship anyway—well, a good portion of it.

I've had more than my share of breakup experience, and it sucks. There is no nice way of breaking up without at least one of you, if not both of you, being upset. You are essentially telling someone that you no longer want him, he's not good enough for you, and you're abandoning him. That hurts.

My job is to make sure that you're an active participant in this event. You need to be a mature, adult woman, to recognize the problems in the relationship, and to make a firm decision. You may have done everything right. You may be an amazing catch. The relationship might not even be "bad." But if three or more months into it the guy still doesn't "get" you, then you can't help the relationship. You can only help yourself. This is the moment when selfish is good.

Women like to tell their friends, "But I *can't* dump him. He'll be *devastated.* And I *love* him." You *can* dump him, and you need to. Yes, he'll be hurt, but that means he loved you in the first place. And things will only get worse if you wait.

Your dumping can be further slowed by those oh-so-exciting rides on the relationship roller coaster: it's good, it's bad, it's oh-so-good again. It's not always easy to know when it's time to get out. In my experience, my biggest breakup weakness is that I don't like to lose; I'm not a quitter. I'll beat that dead horse again and again. But nine times out of ten, flawed relationships are a losing battle.

If you see the problems in the relationship but are still quite conflicted about dropping the ax, here's my advice: Get some distance from the relationship. A few days away, whether on a work-related trip or catching up with the girls, will help you get out of the fishbowl and see the light at the end of the tunnel. You've been miserable for a reason. Relationships are supposed to be 70 percent joy, 30 percent work—not the other way around. If you've decided he's Mr. Wrong, end it.

How to Dump Him

The good news is that it often takes less time to heal if *you* do the dumping. Here's how you do it:

1. Make the breakup abrupt and final. This is going to be difficult if you truly love him, or if you dwell on how close he was to being a great guy. But find some strength and love yourself more than the idea of remaining in a flawed relationship. Bite the bullet and drop the bomb.

2. Give him an honest approximation of why you are breaking up with him, but leave no room for discussion or negotiation over your reasons. It's over.

If He Was a Bad Guy

If he was a jerk, say, "I don't think we should see each other anymore. I had a good time, but this just isn't working for me. I'm not the girl for you, and you're not the right guy for me."

That's it. Don't say anything more, no matter how much he pries. He'll only be prying for selfish reasons to up his game for the next girl. Do not help him by telling him what he needs to "hide" better the next go-around.

If You're Feeling Vindictive

Pity him, wish him good luck, and give him a motherly pat on the back while gently commenting on any weakness in his physical attributes. It's difficult for me to tell you exactly what to say to your particular guy. Pick something you know is a weakness, and comment on it with sympathy—not bitterness—for the most destructive effect. This will drive him nuts—though he may not show it. He'll remember it forever.

If He Was a Good Guy

If he was good, say, "I think we need to break up. I care about you, and I do have love for you, but I'm not in love with you. And I want to be in love. I can't just keep going through the 'motions'—it's not fair to you or to me. I'm sorry."

If You'd Like to Lessen the Blow

Make sure to emphasize the things about yourself that you feel are incompatible with his ways of thinking. Stress that you care about him and that you appreciate all he's done, but that your ideas are different, and as hard as it is to break up right now, it would be worse down the road. You don't want to waste each other's time. Let him know that this is not a spur-of-the-moment emotional decision, but rather one that you have painfully, and with great care, thought about for weeks, and that this is your choice. If you're feeling generous, find something physical about him and say you'll miss it: his arms, the way he kissed, whatever leaves him with a little bit of mojo.

What Not to Do

Big No-Nos
- Do not break up on the phone or via e-mail or text messaging.
- Do not tell him he'll meet another great girl who's right for him.
- Do not wish him good luck.
- Do not show any pity.
- Do not shout back if he gets angry. Just listen and calmly repeat what you've already said when he's done yelling. Guys get angry first, and *then* we hurt.

How to Get Over a Breakup

You're free! Congratulations. You will now endure a week of friends telling you that you'll be happy being alone, or suggesting that you go shopping. They're full of crap. Nothing helps you get over someone like crying and being sad for a while. You're not alone. Bad Boys, bad girls, everyone cries. Lie low and take whatever time you need. It's okay to be miserable when a relationship ends. Your relationship died, and you're mourning. A general rule of thumb is that *it takes one month to heal for every three months you were with someone.*

The first thing you should do is erase his number, his e-mail address, and e-mails. Throw out everything that reminds you of him. *Really.* Throw it out. Unless it was something expensive; that's what yard sales and pawn shops are for.

Women seem to respond to breakups with an obligatory pint of ice cream. I don't really get that, but okay. You could also get profoundly drunk and listen to depression music, though that could have devastating results beyond what you were planning. Or you could take a massive shopping trip, though only the stores benefit from that—and you haven't yet addressed your inner pain.

My suggestion? Go to the gym five days a week, no matter how crappy you feel. And take a long daily walk. Getting your blood pumping will help your mind. Too simple? The best answers in life are simple. Albert Einstein went sailing to clear his head. Movement is a straightforward task, but with oddly calming results.

Still finding your mind heavy with thoughts of your ex, and can't escape? Try writing all those thoughts down in a journal, either as a diary or a letter. You are *emptying* your brain. Then put the journal away. Repeat when necessary.

I think the best way to clear your head is by doing something mundane and routine. Do your job and keep up with your commitments. It takes the pressure off, and before you know it, you'll wake up one day and say, "Wow, I feel . . . fine! Yeah!" A simple physical task that gets you out of the house works. Trust me.

Next up: plan regular nights out with the girls for a flirt-a-thon. Talk to any and every guy in sight, swinging a totally "I couldn't give a shit" attitude. Just have fun. If you end up making out with some random boy toy, all the better.

Then put your game face on. Buy some hot lingerie, and take no prisoners. You're going out in the world to see what's out there for *yourself.* Stop and shop, or hang out everywhere you see men hanging out. Always be ready. Look sexy in the grocery store, the Laundromat, or at your neighbor's BBQ. He'll find you. The new-and-improved you. You're now stronger, smarter, and ready to find your perfect mate.

Chapter 63

Booty Call

Periodically, a failed relationship ends calmly, and both partners emerge with a simple "Oh well, that didn't work [laugh]." For whatever reason, there are no hurt feelings. Maybe you're meant to be friends—friends with benefits, that is.

This is a rare and ideal opportunity on the relationship trail, because you both know each other's tastes, and you hold no grudges. As long as you can truly say that you're *detached* from both the guy and the relationship, and that you're *not* trying to win him back (it won't work), it's time to rename his speed-dial code "Booty Call." Call him when you need a little lovin'.

The best part of this arrangement (well, after the lovin') is that the guy will think you're doing him a favor. Men are brought up to believe that women give sex as a gift, and we find it hard to wrap our minds around the fact that *you* might be using *us*. And, anyway, when it comes to sex, we don't mind being used. Chances are, we'll never figure it out. Your little secret.

Think of this guy as an appliance: turn him on, get him to take you to dinner, let him feel like he's seducing you, and then get what you need. Be selfish—he ain't leaving until you're satisfied. Then shut him off.

The booty call is also a great way to keep your engine warm. Other men will pick up on the fact that you're not desperate, and this can make you more desirable.

There are only two rules to booty calls:

1. Make sure the booty call is done strictly on your terms—*you* make the calls.

2. Choose an expiration date. Write it in your planner in bright red, and stick to it. This ensures that you will eventually move on and cut the physical tie. In general, you should move on as soon as possible.

Bad Boys are adept at keeping the booty call alive for years, so be prepared. We know that women find sex with an ex comfortable, and that it doesn't add another "number" to their lists. We'll try to extend the booty call arrangement by complimenting you frequently and seldom asking you about other guys. We know how to make you feel special, especially given that we know what turned you on in the first place.

The booty call should be used sparingly, and for selfish reasons only. It should be nothing more than a comfy rest area on the speeding highway of relationships—*not* an exit.

Chapter 64

Survival Techniques

Y ou made it. You got out alive. Confirm that you have all your limbs intact, and then move on.

I know that's not always as easy as it sounds. There are lots of clichés to describe being burned by relationships: *Once bitten, twice shy. Fool me once, shame on you; fool me twice, shame on me.* Whenever I reenter the dating pool, I experience two feelings: nausea that's closer to my heart than my stomach, and an overwhelming sense of apathy. *Why should I bother?* I ask myself that same question every time, and sometimes it takes weeks to answer the question. But it comes down to this: you simply don't have any other reasonable choice. Loving relationships are great, and you want to be in one. And the truth is that your last relationship moved you even closer to the prize: true love. Thank that boy for letting you practice on him so that you could be perfect for Mr. Right. All failed experiences will pay off in spades in a future relationship.

Friends will remind you that life changes in a heartbeat, and so will your love life. They'll say things like "Remember, the difference between singleness and coupledom is a simple matter of meeting one person. You can do it!" But how do you get back up on the horse to reenter the dating pool?

Start by thinking about all those athletes who try and fail. They have dedicated their lives to their sport, and they publicly failed, maybe even hurt themselves. The crowd cheers as they limp off to the sidelines, heading back home to regroup, humbly watching their tapes to see what they did wrong. But they let their injuries heal for a few weeks, and then they return to the field. A few months later, they're back out there winning again. If they don't win, they return again and again—as long as it takes to get it right. I expect the same from you, and from myself.

And remember: Men are cheering for you. We want you back out here with us.

Chapter 65

Rebound

In those months of relationship rehab there will be many weeks when you'll want to be alone—and then there will come a time when you'll want to get back up on that horse. That's where I come in.

Here's the deal: There is a period—just after mourning the end of love and before meeting a new man—when you are relationship window-shopping. This period can last a few weeks or several months. Regardless, the rebound period does have a shelf life, so you need to eat it up before it spoils.

Sadly, not all women fresh from a breakup take advantage of the rebound. I've seen a lot of such women bemoaning the fact that they are suddenly single. I understand the pain of heartbreak, but not the chagrin of being single. Don't fight your new status; use it to your advantage! And it can be an advantage . . .

Just for the sake of conversation, let's say there is a crowded room of men, and in a far corner two girls are talking quietly. One girl announces, "I've just gotten out of a long relationship, and I want to start dating." You would suddenly be able to hear a pin drop—before the smart single men flocked to her.

We would flock not because she's *available*, but because we know that she's most likely looking for a rebound guy and won't put pressure on us to become her new boyfriend. She's just gotten out of a relationship, so she doesn't *need* to jump into a new one. But it's not only that. To all the women rebounding from a long relationship, we men salute you with the following compliments:

- You are more confident than the perennially single.
- You are better kissers, and usually better in bed.
- You understand men, and are therefore easier to be around.
- You may not need a rebound guy for very long, but you are a blast to be with while you do.
- What you lack in fashion sense (yes, we all know that the longer the relationship lasts, the lazier we all get) you make up for in being considerate.

You're in an *excellent* situation—you're rebounding! You can make a lot of lemonade with all those relationship lemons. A good rebound is smart and healthy, so start squeezing.

The Right Attitude

In order to enjoy a rebound relationship, however, it is important that you have the right attitude. In most cases, women on the rebound have just the right inner monologue to meet whomever they want and not care if it doesn't work out. I'm talking about the "I don't give a shit" attitude that comes from being freshly released from the chains of a relationship gone bad. This is a rare state of affairs. Although I'm not always happy about being single, when I *am* content, I get more attention than a stripper at a boat show.

The opposite vibe, bitterness or desperation, on the other hand, emits a bad odor. *Pay attention here:* relationships are all about perception—the signals you send out to men when you enter a room, and the way you behave. It's the same for guys. Whether you come off as devil-may-care or bitter will determine whether you end up with a date or not.

Why Bad Boys Make Great Rebound Buddies

At any other time, a Bad Boy will try to control the dating situation. But when a woman is in the rebound stage, she is unbeatable. He can do—or not do—whatever he wants, and she will remain unflappable. It's perfect. An average woman can have her pick of the litter, and you both can have a great time. We just like to have fun, remember? Let's do it together!

What This Means for You

- If you just got out of a relationship, take advantage of not wanting to be in a new one, and date whomever you desire.

- If you are single, feel free to lie and say you just got out of a relationship. This will throw off a guy's game and make it easier for you.

- Rebounding is part of life, so learn to deal with it.

- Rebound times can vary, so take advantage of one while it lasts.

- Next time you're watching a basketball game, look at how hard the men fight for the rebound. Remember that.

- Don't freak out if you start dating like a guy . . . it's normal.

And, if you are rebounding, please contact me directly . . .

Chapter 66
Having Fun

Don't you get it? Boys just wanna have fun. We're overgrown children, and we need to play. Realize that you're dating a big kid—that's who we are. We're goofy, and bringing out that fun side of our personality by mixing a lot of silliness into our dates can only help.

I've been in love a couple of times, and those moments of blissful laughing and being silly were the best times of my life. From my perspective, the humor and silliness were a major reason the relationships worked and lasted. With my big love, Naomi, we used to dance around and have "disco night" in the house. We would pretend we were in a nightclub, playing the roles of the kind of tacky characters you might meet there. First, I would try to pick her up with lame lines (think the *Saturday Night Live* guys) and then she would take on that role. Laugh we did. Fun we had. Nothing keeps love alive like laughter.

Men's tastes are obvious. Look around and see how we occupy our time: games. Whether it's watching football, playing video games, or dancing around and being silly, that's how we spend our leisure time. We like to play the fool.

Do you need further proof that we like silliness? Look at the most popular TV shows men watch: *Family Guy,* the Three Stooges, *South Park, Jackass,* and *Chappelle's Show*—to name a few. And there's an even longer list of movies that most women find inane, but that we love.

When you don't laugh with us, we feel like you don't "get" us. To us you might appear boring, and that's one less thing we have in common. I'm not suggesting that during a romantic dinner you break out with a juggling routine, but you need to find ways to engage us in childlike behavior. Here are some ideas:

Ways to Have Fun with Us Every Day

• Pet names: Every couple has them. If you call him "your big bear," for example, create an entire imaginary world where you take everyday occurrences and relate them to how a bear would be in those exact circumstances. If he comes home from work aggravated, say, "Oh, the bear is angry. Does he want to be left alone in the cave?" This will make him laugh. Bears can also drive, cook, make love, and put the toilet seat down.

• Inappropriate behavior: If you are walking through a mall or are in a restaurant, sing your order to the waiter. Pick a tune you know or make one up.

• The sidewalk talk (one of my favorites): People love to listen in on your conversations when you are walking down the street, so give 'em something to listen to. My specialty? Try breaking out with "No, I'm not keeping your baby. I don't even know if you're the father, and aren't you gay anyway?"

• Sofa silly: Watch one of those damn shows he likes and at least *try* to laugh. Ask him—during a commercial, please— what he thought was the funniest part.

According to a questionnaire I read in *Maxim,* women allegedly consider humor the biggest turn-on. Well? Laughter lightens your heart, takes the pressure off, and makes seeing each other exciting. It's a play date. Duh, isn't it supposed to be fun?

Chapter 67

Arts and Crafty

Men love cute, romantic gestures. They mean you like us. Anything out of the ordinary is wonderful. We may roll our eyes, but deep down we're entertained, and we genuinely appreciate it. We find it adorable and very girly.

I would never forget a girl who wrote me a sexy note on an aluminum pie plate with glued-on pasta. If macaroni isn't your thing, take a look at the list below. If none of these fit your personality, then find the curriculum for a third-grade art class and pick something that suits you.

Romantic Arts-and-Crafts Projects

- Hidden notes: Write little suggestive notes on pieces of paper and hide them where he'll easily find them in his house. Don't put them in places where he could misconstrue that you were snooping in his stuff. Safe bets include on the fridge, in his shoes, under his pillow, and taped to the TV remote.

- Tattoo night: Get a tattoo kit or chocolate paint and draw on each other.

- Chalk outline: Buy some big sticks of sidewalk chalk and write funny things on the street in front of his house—anywhere he might see it. Try to keep these chalky messages in the short-and-sweet category. Remember: it's *chalky*, not *stalky*.

• Food play: Whether you're eating at home or in a restaurant, write things with your food or make dirty pictures (sushi is especially easy to do this with) and show them to him. Another healthy reason to serve up the vegetables: It's amazing what you can do with a carrot and two brussel sprouts. He'll eat it up.

> Note: You might find that you're dating someone who doesn't deserve you. A big indication of this is if he doesn't smile and appreciate your little art project. This could serve as an indicator that he may be the wrong guy. Cut him some slack if he's having a hard day, but otherwise cut him loose!

Arts and crafts should be kept to a limit—say, once or twice a month—so that your gifts are unexpected. You'll keep him thinking, "She's so crazy. I wonder what she'll do next." Trust me, you'll stand out from all the other women he's dated. The girls who have done things like this for me have a special place in my heart, and whenever I think of them I smile.

Encourage him to do the same. I once peed a girl's name in the snow, and I got huge kudos for it. I was just being silly, but she thought it was sweet. By encouraging your man to do things with you that are crafty, you are engaging his "fun bone." And the fun bone's connected to the penis bone, and the penis bone's connected to the love bone . . . You get my point.

Chapter 68

Staying Active

Here comes the easiest, most straightforward relationship fix-it advice you've ever read: a healthy relationship needs motion to have emotion.

As you may remember from Physics 101, *an object in motion tends to stay in motion.* Keep it moving, or there won't be anything there, folks. You can't sit around bored all day and expect things to get interesting come bedtime. Exercise and activity have resounding effects far beyond the intrinsic pleasure of the activity itself. It gets your blood pumping. It gets your hearts working together— and your heart is where love comes from.

You know all the magazine photos of a couple frolicking together? Note that they're *outside.* Though I'll admit to being an avid outdoorsman, I know for a fact that the women I've taken outside for hikes, a kayak paddle, or a swim in a lake have bonded with me. It would be great to meet a woman who could take her own fish off the hook, but that's not important—I will happily de-hook the fish for her. What is important is that the two of us are being active together.

Why? you ask. You city dweller, you suburban mall rat, you nail salon prisoner! *Because doing activities that require trust and physical expression bonds couples.* It just does. Translation: If you're single, get a hobby. If you're involved, try his outdoor passion. If the two of you are "stay-insiders," then it's time to Internet search "outdoor fun."

If you've never played a sport with your partner, why are you holding this book? Get to it. Follow the bouncing ball, whether it's a volleyball, a tennis ball, a football, or just having a ball. No matter where you live, there is fun to be had.

There is only one rule here: Neither person in a couple should attempt to teach the other a sport he or she is already proficient in. Unless you have the patience and skills of the Dalai Lama, leave the lessons to the instructors. I once tried teaching a girlfriend how to snowboard, and it ended in disaster. Nothing is worse than being the entertainment for those on the chairlift as they pass over a crying girlfriend and her boyfriend yelling, "There's *nothing* to be afraid of. Just go down the damn mountain!"

Some safe and highly recommended activities are:

- Catching fireflies: Each person gets a jam jar. Nothing is more fun than running around in the dark like a five-year-old.

- Fishing: Every time I go fishing with a woman, she catches bigger fish than I do. And as long as I take care of the "icky" parts, she's great. If your man likes to fish, have him take you out. If he doesn't, you should both head to the store and get yourself some simple gear and a license, and hit the water.

- Flying a kite: Simple enough, and the two of you can do it together on a beach or in a big field—both great places to spend an afternoon. Or you can get two kites and have kite battles, until the lines are thoroughly intertwined . . .

- Sledding: Don't laugh. Sledding down your local hill is so much fun and so cheap that you shouldn't resist. Buy one of those plastic sleds that will fit two people, sit bobsled style, and fling yourselves down a hill. You'll feel so silly you'll laugh until you cry. As a bonus, running up and down the hill is a great workout. Just make sure you wear deodorant.

Being active together will make you learn about the other person. You'll see him laugh, struggle, and triumph, which will highlight his frustration levels and his ability to be supportive.

A lot of times, couples (me included) fall into "fishbowl" patterns, where they don't interact with the outside world. This not only threatens a relationship, but also limits the fun factor. Outdoor activities get you involved and enjoying life, and provide a great way to see if two hearts really do beat as one.

Chapter 69

Autonomy

No matter how tight you are with your honey, you need to *maintain friends and activities that don't include your partner.* This serves multiple purposes, the most obvious being that if your relationship ends, you'll have your own friends to turn to. Once you lose both a boyfriend and half your friends in a breakup, you'll never make that mistake again.

But more important, your own autonomy in a relationship is *key* to the healthy development of that relationship. All I know is that (scream this next part) it's "nice to be with a woman who has a friggin' life outside of the relationship!"

I get bored very quickly if I can see that the "relationship" is all that my girl is interested in. Too much familiarity in a relationship can sometimes breed a bit of contempt. I want a girl who is so busy

> Note: A girlfriend with no extracurricular activities seems far too "available." Get a life. I *want* to miss you.

with other things that she has to pull herself away because she can't *not* be with me. That is so sexy that I can't even begin to describe how it makes a man feel. But there has to be something to pull yourself away from. A woman just sitting there all the time? Less sexy.

Here's the Bad Boys' conundrum: We love this person, she makes us happy, and she has more good qualities than anyone else we've met, which is why we want to be around her so much. But she doesn't have everything. And neither do we. No one does. No one can stimulate every part of your being, and that's okay. Your significant other cannot be all things to you, nor can you be all things to him. But if both partners are active and involved in other communities, this becomes okay. Outside friends fill in the gaps. You both need to have personal activities that you do separately, be they job-related, a social club (hopefully not a swingers club), or regular exercise classes. This separation builds both trust and lust, and without those two things, you have nothing.

The other problem here is fear, that other four-letter word. Both men and women worry that when our partners are not around, they'll cheat, their feelings will fade, they'll get hurt, or they'll be anally probed by aliens. (We're goofy even in our suspicions, remember?) Our minds play tricks on us when our loved one is off doing his or her own thing. Lighten up. Don't be blind, but start giving your partner the benefit of the doubt.

Oddly enough, in the early stages of writing this book I was dating a woman who always thought my solo activities were "shady." They weren't. I was an angel. (You can stop rolling your eyes, ladies.) But when I stepped outside her line of vision, every event was up for questioning, every friend was suspect, and every missed phone call became a breach. You know what she did? She created a liar. A white liar, but a liar nonetheless. I stopped telling her things because I was sick of listening to the grief. (Ironically, in the end, it was she who was the liar—which is something to consider. If someone doesn't trust you, maybe he's projecting.)

My point is that trust, or the lack thereof, is directly related to autonomy, and is an issue that needs to be addressed by taking sojourns away from each other to stimulate other parts of your psyche. The relationship cannot be either partner's goal in life. Just make sure that your "psyche stimulation" takes place way above your body's Mason-Dixon Line!

Chapter 70

Hunting for Hunting's Sake

Men are hunters by nature. This atavistic hunting trait is primitive—caveman primitive. I'm not an anthropologist, so I'll put it in the terms I know: throughout the relationship, we want to feel, however sporadically, that we're hunting for you. Hunting makes us feel like we're alive. Where do you come in? In every "hunt" there's a fox. You're the fox.

For proof, look to the world of cartoons: Elmer Fudd is still chasing Bugs Bunny for a reason. How boring would *Bugs Bunny* be if Elmer had permanently captured him in the first episode? The cartoon would have lasted two months. Instead, it's been on half a century. Every relationship needs to be "animated." Even after years of marriage, he wants you to tease him and give him a little bit of a hard time. This plays to his innate desire to hunt. It pays to be a "rascally rabbit."

You ladies are not so different in this regard. In my own relationships, when I've given myself up too easily, the woman has become bored. I was *too* easy a catch, and it inadvertently stifled her desire to hunt. Actually, women call it "chasing," but it's the same thing. We all like a little challenge.

The question, of course, is: How do you maintain a hunting atmosphere over a long period of time? Easy: spontaneity. By being spontaneous with how and when you'll get frisky, you'll keep a man on his toes. Long after you've become "his," he'll still be on the prowl. He likes this.

There is only one rule here: you don't want to withhold sex or be too coy too often. That becomes frustrating. Men don't like frustration. They like suspense, followed soon after by winning. Instead, tantalize just enough to keep him alert and ready.

Adjust this principle depending on how aggressive your man is. The more aggressive he is, the more spontaneous you need to be. The less aggressive, the more laid-back you can be. For Bad Boys, the trick is to act like Houdini with your availability . . . now you see it, now you don't. We're so used to getting action whenever we want that a girl's unpredictability drives us "happily" nuts. Our agenda is to figure out her pattern of behavior so we can do the least amount of work with the greatest reward. Oddly, *the more work we do, the more invested we are.* Before you know it, you'll have us chasing you.

I'll tell you a secret: sometimes I hunt just for the sake of hunting. I want to see what it takes to get a woman. Seduction, not sex, is the motivation. Am I able to seduce her? Am I able to figure out what makes her tick? The women who keep me guessing are also the ones who keep me in a relationship. A physically confident woman with a shining personality who *also* makes me hunt sits at the pinnacle of the relationship mountain. She is queen.

A man's desire to hunt is a law of nature that isn't going away. It applies to all men. Even if you've been married for years, it would behoove you (oooh, big girly word) to keep that dog hunting, sniffing around trying to figure you out.

People are always comparing men to dogs, but why not also compare them to cats? Have you ever seen a cat with a mouse? The cat doesn't just pounce on the little rodent and kill it; it stalks its prey, captures it, and plays with it a while before it eats it.

Aren't you glad you're reading a book written by a man with all these gross and graphic analogies? But just in case you're too grossed out to get the point, I asked my friend Arianne to chime in. She says, "Yes, rather than the touching Rodent Death example, let's try imagining the cutest pooch you've ever seen, a fluffy poof-ball named Truffles. Truffles is fetching a stuffed animal that you've thrown through the air. The dog will run after that stuffed animal no matter how many times you throw it, and come back happily panting, toy in mouth. Truffles will play this game five days a week for his entire life, despite living with the toy and knowing perfectly well that he could play with it at any point. Truffles will be even more thrilled if you throw the stuffed animal into some bushes, or fake her out, or tuck some treats into the stuffed animal. But if you make it too hard—say, throwing the toy onto a car roof—Truffles will pout and give up. Truffles may instead go play with the neighbors.

"Truffles is Steve. He wants the stuffed animal badly, and the more interesting you make it, the bigger a smile you'll get from Steve. This is how all men are. They like to always play the game, and to always win the game."

You just have to provide the game.

Chapter 71

Housebreaking the Beast

Yoiu're with a guy who gets your heart pumping and your thighs shaking. He's a little *bad*, not quite a Bad Boy. He feels *right*. And he appears to be in love with you. You should be thrilled. You've got a trophy, and you're all ready to stuff him and mount him on the wall. But is that little "doomsday voice" in your head thinking that this stud won't stay in the stable for long? Is he too good to be true?

It's at this point in the relationship that women attempt to domesticate the beast. You're in the "cohabitating" stage, whether officially or unofficially, and he needs to be a good roommate and boyfriend. No more unexplained disappearances, no more checking out other women. So you create rules: dinner times, bedtimes, regular phone calls. The beast doesn't like this. The beast thinks, "WTF?"

Let me help you. You don't want to throw your baby out with the bathwater. All you need to do is housebreak him, not give him a lobotomy. Even the strongest wild animal can be broken in, with time and with training. Men are the same way, but when you're done, you still want him to run free and keep a little of his wild side—nice to have in the bedroom. Isn't that the magnet that pulled you in?

He needs to keep enough of his old badass self to keep you enchanted, but also to lose the irresponsibility and the will to philander. He needs to make a lasting commitment to you, which involves not checking out your girlfriends, not disappearing for nights on the town, and not secretly keeping in touch with his ex-girlfriends, as well as being a good responsible person to live with.

You want to know how to achieve that? How much will you give me? Oh, right. You bought this book, so I owe you.

Your overall strategy should be to domesticate him by making it seem like it's something you are doing together, and not just his chore. From the first moment of cohabitation, let him believe that this is kind of new for you, too, like it's a project that you will work on together for the common good.

Not quite sure what to change and what to keep? To help you narrow it down, write out a list of things that you love about him. On that same piece of paper write down what you want changed. Next, write down the things that you could live with if he didn't change them and the things that you just couldn't allow, the deal breakers. Now that you can look at it in black and white, make mental notes of the top six things you'd like to change. And then throw out that piece of paper. You would never want him to find it. Next time you have a talk, bring up one of the things you'd like him to consider changing, and ask if there is anything he would like you to improve on. Slowly whittle down your list until he's in good shape.

Best Friend

This whole process will be much easier if he becomes your "best friend." (See Chapter 50 for instructions.) Still feeling like a girlfriend and not a best friend? Tear down that wall by being a "guy's girl," making it impossible for him to ever think, "It's a guy thing; she'll never understand." So few women seem to totally "get" us that at times we feel isolated in a relationship. This may require you to do some research in the form of observing men in their natural environment, reading what they read, watching what they watch, and, to a certain extent, putting yourself in their shoes—minus the peeing standing up.

Think of him as your little sociology project for a couple of weeks. This should shed some light on who he is and why he acts the way he does, putting you in a much better position to correctly interpret his actions.

Q&A

Q: You can't *really* change a man, can you?

A: You can change a man's habits, but not who he is. The easiest thing to change is the way *you* respond to him. This will cause a chain reaction, and eventually his behavior will change. I can assure you of this from personal experience: I've been very bad, and have been changed by the right woman several times in my life. For example, let's say your man constantly loses things, and always ropes you into his searching panic. You can't stop him from losing things, but you can simply ignore him by continuing with what you were doing and not dropping everything to help him search. Your lack of response will teach him. If you don't like it, don't respond.

Playing House

Playing house is especially fun for men if we feel that we are only "playing" house. It's a sneaky but legitimate way for women to get us comfortable with the idea. The first time I moved in with a girl, I was petrified: *Oh my God, this was serious. Like marriage. Commitment.* But the woman I was with was so playful, fun, and supportive that I fondly remember our living together and can't wait to find a woman to do it with again for the long term. Going home to her at night was *fun.*

One of her cleverer strategies was to not judge me. Oh, she was strict about certain things: I had to lose the "little black book," no upright toilet seats, no piling up the dishes, and a mandatory one night a week where we did something special and romantic, just the two of us. But she would *talk* to me if she was disappointed, not *name-call* and get dramatic.

All in all, you have to feel your way through the domesticating process, take it slow, and keep him to his promises. Before you know it, you'll be out in front of your home, painting that white picket fence.

Part VI

Q&A

You may be saying, "But Steve, what about my particular situation? It's different, and I don't know what to do!" Well, then this part of the book is for you. Over the years I've shelled out tons of advice to women, and from that, I've chosen ten specific questions/situations and their responses. I picked these particular questions for a very simple reason: they—and variations of them—were some of the most frequently asked questions.

I must admit, when it came to narrowing it down to just ten questions, it was difficult. I want you to understand how, and why, I chose the questions I did. First off, let me explain my methodology: I drank heavily, taped hundreds of questions to a wall, and started throwing darts. Don't you dare roll your eyes. It's a very scientific method and one I'm sure that Stephen Hawking employs on a regular basis—albeit, a dangerous one: I ruined my wall, started a small fire when I hit an electric cord, and one of the darts flew out of my apartment window. (I heard screams outside but quickly shut off the lights and hit the floor. No one caught me.)

On a more serious note, no matter how many questions I chose or what subjects I selected to cover, I knew someone, somewhere, might feel left out. However, you haven't been abandoned; get in touch with me at www.askstevesantagati .com, keep your question(s) as short and to-the-point as possible, and I'll answer them. In the meantime, I hope some of the following questions reach out to you. You're *not* alone.

Troubleshooting Q&A

Q: I'm a single mom with two kids. Guys freak out about this. Plus, I'm often exhausted from raising these little hellions and don't have the energy to get all dolled up. What to do?

A: Set aside time just for you to do things that make you feel pretty and feminine, whether it's exercising, manicures, or shopping. You work hard, and you deserve it. And stop worrying that your kids are a dating problem, because they're only a hindrance if you make them a hindrance. A guy will feel comfortable with your children when he clearly sees that you are not expecting to burden him with some other guy's kids. Of course, because you're a single mom, you need to go slowly, but your dating life can be as hoppin' as you want it to be.

Q: Why can men in general not handle an aggressive woman?

A: Men can't handle aggressive women for several reasons:

- They feel emasculated by women who seem more confident than they are. In general, you want to avoid these men, because you won't like them anyway.

- They like to feel that they are pursuing or hunting you, and if you are too aggressive or available, it takes that away from us. The effect is similar to when a man is too much all over you—it's a turnoff.

- If a woman is aggressive in the wrong place and at the wrong time (at work or in public), he may get embarrassed, even though in general he likes how she acts.

Overall, you want to be a little aggressive if that's in your nature (personally, I love strong, aggressive women!), and then let him come to you. Don't deny a man his desire to hunt you down. If you're in a relationship, it's okay to be aggressive sometimes, but play a little bit of "cat and mouse." Men love that!

Q: I'm "hanging" with a guy who's sleeping with another girl, and he tells me about it. Please tell me that I am stupid.

A: That's a double-edged sword. It's great that he's told you, so now you know and you can bail out. But it kind of sucks, because now you have to bail out and feel a certain amount of rejection. The headline? You win! Why? Because you know. He told you. So you're lucky. Most guys will not tell women about the other action they have on the side.

You could also attempt to become a Black Widow. Check out Chapter 47, "Black Widows." And use condoms.

Q: Hola! I'm twenty-four and from Wisconsin. I have a problem with being attracted to emotionally unavailable men. What do I do?

A: Being attracted to men who are emotionally unavailable is normal. They're not easy to get, and that's why you like them. The "nice guys" bore you. Instead, you want to find a decent guy who has an "edge," and herein lies the dilemma. Such guys aren't easy to find. In the meantime, remember this: you're as in charge as you want to be. Look as hot as you can, and carry yourself with an inner monologue of "I'm hot, and I don't give a fuck." You'd be surprised at how attractive that is to men.

Guys your age are tough to pin down. They are going crazy inside, and all they want to do is get some action. You're that action, and that's your power. Keep it like a carrot on a stick for as long as possible. It's like fishing: once you have one on the line, play him a little so he doesn't "spit" the hook or break off. And, as always, be proactive in dating. Take charge!

Q: Why is it so difficult for men to communicate? Are you a psychologist?

A: I'm not a psychologist. If I were, I would know very little about the real world of relationships and dating. I learned the real way.

It's not always "difficult" for guys to communicate. Instead, what you're seeing is probably the result of years of former communication-gone-wrong experiences. He probably once tried to tell a girl how he felt about something, and she either went nuts or misinterpreted what he was trying to say. Or, even worse, he once opened up to a girl about how much he liked her, and she dumped him. Once bitten, twice shy. So he has learned from his experiences and now figures that he just won't bother. Another possibility is that he *thinks* he's communicating. Men and women say the same things but in a different language.

If you've got a guy who won't talk, the best thing you can do is let him concretely know that you love blunt people. Be blunt with him on a few choice topics to open up the new communication ground. But get ready, because opening the communication flood-gates always brings some funky stuff floating down that river of honesty, and if your man is not the most sophisticated fish in the sea, he may inadvertently say some mean things. The best thing to do is to keep him on a specific topic.

Q: I always tell my girlfriends who are having trouble with their men, "Listen, if you find yourself crying and wondering why all the time . . . MOVE ON!" What do you think about my philosophy?

A: Your philosophy is a good Band-Aid, and sound advice. But it doesn't cure the problem. By a certain age you know men, but do you know yourself? Are you still attracting the same kinds of men by putting out the same "ad"?

My philosophy is for women to be more proactive in the dating world, to go out and take charge with the best men they can imagine, while understanding how men think. Tell your girlfriends to stay hot and sexy, and to think of themselves as flowers: the brightest and the best attract the most bees . . . and have the best chances of getting pollinated.

Q: Do you think a very jealous person will ever trust someone and back off in a relationship? Or do you believe that jealousy becomes a way of life and is carried into all relationships? Impress me here!

A: Jealousy is insecurity. Weak people tend to be jealous more than strong people, though we all feel a little jealous from time to time. It really depends on how old the jealous person is. If he is old and set in his ways, good luck—chances are he won't change. I suggest sitting the person down and saying, "Here's a reality check for you. We can't, nor do we want to, be around each other twenty-four hours a day. If we don't have trust in our relationship, we have nothing. Without trust, my relationship with you is no different than my relationship with a complete stranger." Engage in activities with that person that encourage his trust, but don't baby him. When he is untrusting for no reason, tell him to chill out. If he continues, recommend therapy. You're his lover, not his shrink.

One more note on jealousy: we all like a little bit of jealousy, because it means that your partner likes you and cares about you. Jealousy is not all bad. Treat it like junk food: you should "eat" very little!

Q: I meet someone, date him, love him, then leave. What's my problem? Will I ever commit?

A: You're funny—and you have dater's ADD. Maybe you don't have a problem. Maybe you're not cut out for long-term relationships, or maybe you haven't met the right guy, or are dating the wrong type. Do you want to commit? Have you ever committed? It's nice being in love with the right person; it's fun, the sex is steady (at least at my house), and you get to know someone. But the truth is, any decent relationship is work, and if you have a job that keeps you super busy, then a relationship may be a chore. Ask yourself this: *What is it you really want?*

Q: Five years ago, due to self-esteem issues I had an affair. That's what my husband and everyone else would call it. I call it fate. In my heart I thought I had found the person whom I believed I should have been with all my life. I believe God had a hand in our meeting and being together. I was so unhappy that I think he came into my life to make me happy again, and I was happy as long as I was with him. Then I would have to go back to my real life again. I couldn't stand the fact I was lying to everyone and I tried to end it several times only to go back to seeing him because I missed him so much. My husband got my password changed to my e-mail and found out about us. Everything came to a halt. We haven't seen each other since. That was five years ago. My husband forgave me, and we still live together. The other man's wife forgave him, and they still live together. I have accepted the fact that he is with her. What I can't figure out is why! And why did he break my heart? And why do I still have some feelings for him? I was unhappy and on the road to divorce before I met him. I told him up front that I wanted to be with him. I don't think he ever felt that way about me. So why did he have anything to do with me in the first place? I think he truly loved me, just differently from how he loved his wife. Our love was so exciting!

I was just hoping you could help me see the side of him I never knew—the side that chose to give me up.

A: Although I may not have the "exact" answer, I can, at least, give you my opinion—and, if nothing else, something to think about. Okay, here we go. Fact: relationships take a lot of work—as you know. But being with the same person day in and day out can—and usually does—become boring: the sex drops off, the affection drops off, and spontaneity vanishes. In comes a guy who is sexy and wrong: voilà . . . you're alive again! I've been that "wrong guy" (Bad

Boy stuff). You have to sneak around; his body is new to you, and yours to him. Mmmm. Fun. I'm not saying I condone affairs. I'm just saying that I understand their allure. I've never been married, but I've had flings with separated women. So you jump in and keep everything quiet. It's very exciting! But eventually someone gets careless and someone gets hurt. When people ask me if they should have an affair, I always tell them no. A one-night stand where there is no way anyone will ever find out (meaning you are far from home and practice safe sex) . . . well, that's up to you. But affairs are messy. Do the math: the shorter the fling, the less chance of getting caught or attached. My overall philosophy is to try to work it out with the guy you're with, and if you've exhausted all avenues, break it off with them and *then* go find a new guy.

Why did he break your heart? I don't know the guy or his side of the story, but here are some possibilities (and hopefully he wasn't careless but, instead, breaking your heart was a very tough decision!):

1. He felt guilty and now he has to make it up to his wife by staying with her. (He feels that he "owes her.") He may have lost his lust for his wife but not his love. Understandable.

2. It's also a distinct possibility that he's afraid—meaning, he knows what he has with his wife, but with you the future is uncertain. Personally I find that boring, but then again, I'm not married—for that reason, among many others.

3. Divorce would have cost him a lot of money and problems, including custody issues and family ridicule.

4. He probably did love you and still thinks about you but considers the ROI (return on investment) too low. In other words, you're amazing, but having a relationship with you just isn't worth it because of all the complications.

5. Finally, he may have grown tired of the affair. Only you and he can answer that. Did you spend your last moments in the heat of passion before it blew up? If so, chances are it's possibilities 1–4 and not 5.

Guys love to have a new woman in their lives. We love to fantasize, and only a new woman/new naked body can get that going. Why do you think men look at porn? But we have a romantic side, too. We like to wonder what a relationship would be like if we chose someone else. A new woman treats us differently. You're lucky. You and he have both remained with your original partners. If your sex life feels dead with your husband, you need to make attempts to get it going again. If that fails, then you need to do whatever you feel is right. Life is short, and sitting around miserable for even a moment is not good—so work it out or get out of it! The side of him that gave you up is the side of him that is "safe" or guilty. Chances are it has little to do with you. I've met dozens of hot women in my life, but the aggravation and extraneous heartache attached to a possible relationship with them just wasn't worth it, so I moved on. It's a tough choice to make. But to keep it simple I chose not to do it.

Q: Hey smarty pants, I just saw you on some show. So you're a relationship expert, huh? Okay, well, I just looked in my boyfriend's cell phone and he's been calling his ex-girlfriend. He told me they were done and not communicating. I'm freaked out now because if he knows I was looking, he'll turn it into a trust issue. And, of course, I don't know what they're talking about. Plus, she lives far away. My question is: Was it bad that I looked in his phone, and what should I do now that I know?

A. Yes, it's bad that you looked in his phone. Why? Because you may be freaking out over nothing. That, and you violated his privacy. Maybe he sneaked behind your back because he figured you would make a big scene if he told you he was talking to his ex. Guys hate drama. His conversations could very well have been innocent.

But for the moment, let's say he's guilty and he's flirting with his ex. I suggest you wait a week, don't look in his phone again, keep your mouth shut, and then talk about an ex of your own. Say how he called you (make it up if you have to) and how it's inevitable that certain people from our past will call us. Say that you think couples should be mature about this. If he doesn't come clean at that moment, then store it, because he may be waiting until he's comfortable. If in a day he doesn't come clean, ask him if he ever talks to his ex. Say you won't be mad. He won't believe you, but say it anyway. If he still doesn't come clean, I would mentally start the separation process, because he's clearly got something to hide. In general, I don't recommend looking in anyone's phone unless it's an emergency situation.

Epilogue

Playing it safe isn't what it's cracked up to be. In the dating world, the greater the risk, the greater the gain, and if you don't put yourself out there, you will suffer a life of humdrum boredom. Don't do it! Overcome your fear! It's okay to be worried and afraid, and sometimes rejected. Do it anyway!

So what does all this have to do with wrapping up *The Manual*? Everything. I wrote this book because I believe in going after life proactively, with total abandon. From this moment, think of yourself and relationships in a new light. Take whatever baby steps you need, and then keep moving forward.

Be proactive. Go after the man you want. Be smart about it. Let rejection sting and then roll off your back, but *keep moving forward.* Be culpable and honest with yourself. And always remember that you deserve to be in a relationship just as much as that sappy couple walking hand in hand on the beach. There's a bucket of sap out there with your name on it. Now you have the knowledge to tap it.

Good Luck. xoxo

Steve

Acknowledgments

It irks me when celebrities pull out the *note* from their formal wear and begin thanking an enormous list of people whom none of us regular folk have ever heard of; it makes no sense to do that on television. Boring! However, in print, you have the choice to read this or flip the page, and I, of course, don't have to worry about the "music" coming on to kick me off the "acknowledgments page." So here is the list of people (in no particular order) without whose help the success of this book would not have been possible.

The Oscars go to:

- Selina Cicogna (a publicist and friend)—for getting me the appointment to pitch my book! Cool.

- Rachael Ray (some chick who cooks for a living)—for helping me with the negotiation process, and giving me the confidence to write the book I wanted to write and not overthinking it: "Just write the damn book, Steve."

- Kristin Kiser (bigwig Editorial Director at Crown)—for buying my book, listening to my naughty stories, and believing in me.

- Shana Drehs (my editor)—for being the most amazing, patient, clearheaded, nurturing, and incredibly wonderful editor in the world. This was my first book, and Shana had to do a bit of "hand holding" at times. I was agentless and had no prior experience with the book-writing process, and Shana created an environment that made writing a blast! We should all be so lucky to get a Shana on our first book.

• Arianne Cohen (my "gun for hire" editor)—for keeping me focused, cracking the whip, and knowing when to "edit" me and when to let me run with it. I learned a ton from Arianne . . . so I guess it's true: Harvard girls are really naughty. I will now go forward with aplomb (wink).

• Laura Duffy (art director)—for not rolling her eyes (in front of me) when I demanded my picture be on the cover.

• Lindsey Moore (editor who likes to party)—for picking up the ball and keeping things from getting "hairy." LOL!

• Courtney McCraw (aka "little marcher" . . . always there for me)—for listening, helping, loving, and punching me (ya did so punch me!). Court was, and is, a very important part of my life.

• Lisa Dallos (publicist, friend, and Austrian Stick Dance Champion)—for getting me in doors that would never have been open, for hanging up on me over and over again, for treating me to dinner when I was broke, for challenging me to be the best, for rolling her eyes and laughing at my stories, for launching this book into the public eye.

• Claude Hillel (Clode)—for letting me sleep on his couch (in a tiny one-bedroom) for close to a year, listening to me complain about TV politics, and getting my ass in the gym.

• All television producers and magazine editors (you know who you are)—for supporting me by having me on your shows and quoting me in your mags!

• Me (Bad Boy)—for never giving up, never apologizing for who I am, and having the balls to live and die by my own sword. And, of course, for being bad.

Printed in the United States
by Baker & Taylor Publisher Services